What others are saying about

Help, I'm Stuck With These People for the Rest of Eternity!

Christian Advice on Healthy Relationship Characteristics and Making Relationships Work

I0088385

"Once again, Sue Gaddis has done an excellent job in communicating what is still the most central theme of the New Testament epistles—loving one another. Where there's little love, there's much junk! Read this book!"

ROD AND JULIE ANDERSON

THE PRAYER FOUNDATION, LONDON

"Because the kingdom of God is first relational, then functional, and thirdly doctrinal, Susan has touched the core. As go our families, so goes the church. It is vital that we gain the ability to resolve conflict and 'walk together in agreement' (Amos 3:3). This tool is critical—we have to get this 'loving your brother' thing down. Susan, through her many years of personal experience and gifted application, gives us a practical guide."

GARY GOODELL

THIRD DAY CHURCHES, INC.

"Susan's book speaks into the primary issue of Christianity—relationships. Jesus' prayer in John 17, plus the first and second commandments, are all relational. With divorce and church splits rampant in the church, we need help. Thank God, Susan gives us practical ways to be doers of the Word!"

RICK AND PAM WRIGHT

THE GATHERING PLACE, NORTH HOLLYWOOD, CALIFORNIA

"Susan Gaddis is a woman of excellence and honesty who gives real life experiences of other people as well as her own to help you and I to have godly relationships. Susan simply unfolds the Scriptures and brings it down to a level we can all relate to and understand. I highly recommend *Help, I'm Stuck With These People For the Rest of Eternity!*, for all pastors, leaders, or anyone who desires to live as Christ."

REV. PAT CHEN

FOUNDER, FIRST LOVE MINISTRIES

INTERNATIONAL PRAYER CENTER

HARVEST CHURCH PASTORAL STAFF

"The church needs this book! Susan Gaddis has done a masterful job at applying God's Word to relationships using real-life examples to which everyone can relate. Her wisdom, exhortation, and sound counsel bring conviction to those genuinely seeking to be transformed into Christ's image."

PASTORS ROB AND MARY LEE

ACTS CHRISTIAN FELLOWSHIP, TORONTO, CANADA

HELP,

I'M STUCK

WITH THESE PEOPLE

FOR THE REST OF ETERNITY!

CHRISTIAN ADVICE ON HEALTHY RELATIONSHIP
CHARACTERISTICS AND MAKING RELATIONSHIPS WORK

By Susan Gaddis

**ETERNAL
FOUNDATIONS**
Resources for Building a Spiritual Legacy

Eternal Foundations Curriculum

www.eternalfoundations.com

Copyright © 2004 by Susan Gaddis

All rights reserved. Published 2004

ISBN: 978-1-932505-19-1

Printed and bound in the United States of America

First edition: 2004

Second edition: 2011

Cover design by Design 7 Studio

This book is dedicated to my husband, Tom.

Grow old along with me
The best is yet to be . . .
~Robert Browning

Contents

It's All About Me!

It's All About Them!

It's All About Us!

Part One

It's All About Me!

Chapter 1

Eternity In My Heart

"He has made everything beautiful in its time. Also He has put eternity in their hearts" (Ecclesiastes 3:11 NKJV).

Huge, billowy clouds overshadowed what scant blue sky was left beyond the treetops of the cemetery. Raindrops were starting to fall as I hurried to find Karali's grave among the aged markers. The old cemetery was small and isolated in the rural Adelaide area of Paso Robles. She had only been buried for a few months and her marker would be the lone new one. No one was around. Why was this so difficult?

Karali had been the worship leader at our church for some time. My husband had led her to the Lord years ago and we had watched her mature in her Christian life. After high school, she married a wonderful Christian man and they had two lovely children. Her death was sudden and unexpected—a scuba diving accident. It had hit me hard, and visiting her burial place was important to me. I needed closure.

I found the grave in the back of the cemetery. Grieving, I stood and stared at the new marker that had begun to sink into the ground. The heavy rains had left their gloomy influence on the whole scene. Caught up in my own anguish, I almost missed the still, small voice that had begun to speak. Accommodating my dullness, the Lord spoke louder and with authority, "Why do you seek the living among the dead?"

I stood corrected. Karali was not there. Yes, we had experienced a temporary separation, but our relationship was an eternal one.

We would reconnect sometime in the future. My friend wasn't dead. She was alive and living in a far greater reality than mine. She would continue to grow and experience all that God had originally designed life to contain. Karali was on the greatest adventure of her life and I was still stuck on planet Earth to live out my days in anticipation of what she was already experiencing. I would miss her, but what stories we would have to tell when we again meet! For me, *eternity* became a reality on that day, thirteen years ago.

Most Christians have a limited view of life. They see themselves pursuing a career, raising a family, and eventually retiring. Through it all, they endeavor to faithfully serve the Lord in whatever capacity they can. This, however, is not the scriptural view of the Christian life! God's perspective looks at our life here on Earth as "here today and gone tomorrow." It is a very short time in contrast to the eternal scheme of things that He has planned for us. It is the place where we come to know Him and begin to be transformed into the image of the Son. Our relatively short life span is simply the starting point for the rest of life that He has designed for us in the ages to come.

The context of our present existence and the future is the kingdom of God. It envelops all that is eternally significant. It is the place where we eternally relate to the Lord and to each other. This kingdom is what connects Earth and Heaven. That is why the only two things that translate from this world into the next are the eternal Word of God and our relationships with other people. They are the only things we can take to Heaven with us! Frank B. Minirth, MD and Paul D. Meier, MD put it well when they said in their book, *Happiness Is a Choice*:

> A healthy perspective is to realize that only two tangible things will last forever—the Word of God and people. In Matthew 24:35, we read, 'Heaven and Earth shall pass away, but my words shall not pass away.' In 2 Peter 3:10, we find everything else will eventually be destroyed. A healthy perspective is to invest our lives in the only two things that have eternal significance— The Word of God and people.[i]

Because we are people who are stuck together for the rest of eternity, we might as well get used to it and learn how to properly relate to each other here and now! Eternal relationships are what the Scriptures are all about. The Bible is mostly a textbook about relationships. It talks of how man is to relate to God and how we are to relate to one another. Many of us look to the Scriptures as a book of doctrine, but fail to realize that it is also a how-to instruction manual for eternal relationships. Our lives show the results of our ignorance.

Ignorance on display

My friend stood there with tears running down her face. Apparently, some well-meaning Christian had told her that her husband wouldn't have died if she had prayed for him more. It didn't matter that we both knew this was immaturity talking; she still felt devastated.

At the time of this writing, I have been in pastoral ministry for 28 years. During this time, I have observed the inconsistency of the people of God in applying the scriptural instructions for relationships. I, too, have often been one of these people. These instructions aren't learned overnight or in a vacuum—they require study and application in the day-to-day pressures of life. This isn't fun, and it isn't easy!

In the past, the Greek way of learning required only the obtaining of information and knowledge. A man was considered wise by how much knowledge and philosophy he could articulate. However, the Hebrew idea of wisdom never separated knowledge from application. It didn't matter how much a person knew; what mattered was how much he had applied of what he knew.

Many Christians have accepted the Greek way of understanding knowledge, but have never embraced the Hebrew concept of wisdom. Such believers would readily agree to everything taught in this book and could probably teach it to others. But, when it comes to application, these same people frequently excuse and justify why they don't have to obey relational Scriptures.

Our church contains people who have been active in ministry in other churches, yet are wounded because of improper handling of relationships, both by themselves and by those with whom they ministered. We also have within our midst those who have lost marriages and families to poor relationship skills. Others become a part of our church family and begin to move out in ministry, yet continue to demonstrate how little they know about scriptural principles of interrelating. Many of these people have been believers for a long time. Unfortunately, what we are experiencing is common in most churches.

Sam had been involved in worship for many years. However, he was having a hard time adjusting to the style of music the new worship leader was introducing to the church. "I also think he has no right to suggest we practice more during the week," Sam told the other members of the worship team. "This team has always done fine with the way we have been doing worship and our practice times are as much a time of fellowship as they are preparing for Sunday service." It wasn't long before discord was spread throughout the church. By the time Sam and the new worship leader sat down to process their differences, the resentment was too high for a mutually satisfying resolve to the conflict. Sam eventually moved on to another church along with some of his supporters.

No wonder churches wound people and go through church splits. Our reputation in the world does not line up with the criteria that, "By this all men will know that you are my disciples, if you love one another" (John 13:35 NIV). In many cases we act worse than those we are trying to reach with the Gospel! This is why this book was written. Its purpose is to train God's people in the ways of kingdom relationships and to release them into accountability for the actions that go with this knowledge.

God purposely places us in relationship with other people. He gives us spouses, children, friends, and a church family. Those close to us see us at our worst. They are often the ones who push our buttons and bring to the surface what is operating as our old sin nature. Sometimes they hurt us, yet they are also the ones who love us the most. Close relationships can be instrumental in encouraging the fragile and dormant areas of our lives to bloom and grow strong. They also can be helpful in rubbing the sharp points off of our personalities. "As iron sharpens iron, so one man sharpens another" (Proverbs 27:17 NIV).

I thought I was a pretty mature Christian until I got married. Living by myself, I assumed that I was an experienced believer. Being engaged to a future pastor only seemed to confirm it in my mind. My illusions popped as the pressures of married life began to expose the immature characteristics still residing within me. It didn't take long to realize that there was still some ugly sin nature stuff left in my life. Having children only magnified the problem. I now know that having a family is God's secret agenda for surfacing all our *yuck* so He can deal with it. By giving me six children, He made it real clear that He meant business!

Family disunity, divorce, the breaking of friendships, and church-hopping are common in the American culture. They are indications that people do not understand the kingdom principle of a commitment to process relationship problems. Relationships are not easy; they take work. We have to know God's instructions, practice them, and constantly rely on the power of the Holy Spirit.

This doesn't mean that we will never experience family disunity, the end of friendships, or the need to change churches. Relationships always involve at least two people and each must make their own decisions. Disunity usually results when one party doesn't want to learn or practice God's instructions for relationships. Occasionally, we must end relationships that are destructive. This, however, should be the exception and not the rule for Christians.

Processing relational problems is not an option in the kingdom of God. Jesus expects us to deal with the issues that irritate us and lead us to separate ourselves from others. We are not allowed to just end a friendship or reject a person because they have become an uncomfortable commodity. It is true that there are boundaries in relationships, but God institutes boundaries

15

for protection and safety, not as a form of rejection. The kingdom of God will always require us to work on our relationships.

Welcome to the kingdom

"I'm not angry, I'm just intense! I've always been this way and she knew that when she married me," Jim exclaimed in a tight voice. His wife deflated back into her chair. This counseling session wasn't going as well as I had hoped.

It took quite a while for Jim (names have been changed to protect the guilty) to understand that his intensity was a form of anger and that his marriage was suffering because of his intensity. It didn't matter what he had been like when he and his wife married. What mattered was what he was becoming. I also wasn't buying into the fact that just because he was Italian, he had a cultural right to communicate with his non-Italian wife in a forceful manner. His family culture had been superseded by a new family culture when he became a believer.

When you become a Christian you automatically find your citizenship transferred from Satan's kingdom to the kingdom of God. "For He delivered us from the domain of darkness, and transferred us to the kingdom of His beloved Son" (Colossians 1:13 NASB).

This kingdom is eternal. It will never end. What you learn as a citizen of this kingdom will continue to be operational in your life when you step from this Earth onto Heaven's terra firma. You are an eternal person and you exist with others who are also eternal people. Together, we are learning how our new homeland of the kingdom operates so that we might be citizens that rightly represent our King. Some of our fellow citizens are no longer available to communicate with us, as they have taken up residence in another location—Heaven. However, they are still alive and active people with whom we will share eternity future.

Every kingdom has a location. The kingdom of God is located in the hearts and minds of men and women who have made Jesus Christ their King. This includes those who walk on Earth

16

and those who walk in Heaven's domain. Wherever the King is, there is the kingdom. The kingdom of God includes literal territory in heavenly places and wherever Jesus is acknowledged as Lord on Earth. At some point in the future, a completely new Heaven and Earth will replace the old and they will become the territorial realm of God's kingdom.

Each kingdom has a culture and the kingdom of God is no exception. It has laws, a system of organization, and principles of operation, all of which are recorded throughout the Bible. It has its own language—one spoken by a renewed mind and seasoned with truth and grace. This kingdom culture is rich in righteousness, joy, and peace—the hallmarks of the kingdom of God. No religious, gloomy or somber mood is allowed where the King rules and reigns! Permeating the atmosphere are love, joy, peace, patience, goodness, kindness, faithfulness, gentleness, and self-control.

> For the kingdom of God is not a matter of eating and drinking, but of righteousness, peace and joy in the Holy Spirit (Romans 14:17 NIV).

> You will show me the path of life; in Your presence is fullness of joy; at Your right hand are pleasures forevermore (Psalm 16:11 NKJV).

> But the fruit of the Spirit is love, joy, peace, patience, kindness, goodness, faithfulness, gentleness and self-control. Against such things there is no law (Galatians 5:22-23 NIV).

The culture of the kingdom of God is something we will be adjusting to throughout our life here on Earth. It is radically different from the culture of the world that we have experienced for so long. Our struggles with people are most evident when we find ourselves operating according to the mores of our old world experience rather than the principles of God's kingdom. Accordingly, God places us in many different relationships so we can begin to practice kingdom culture.

As eternal people, we need to be committed to the relationships that God has placed in our lives. This includes the commitment to process any problems that threaten to bring separation.

17

Unsaved people need our commitment so that they can learn about the King and His kingdom. Those that are saved are people with whom we will be spending eternity future. Relating with others isn't always a heavenly experience! Learning to graciously co-exist in the kingdom takes time. By learning the ways of the kingdom, we become transformed into the image of the King and we experience transformed relationships.

Supernatural transformation

Leo and Jenny had been married for eleven years when they finally decided to get a separation. They struggled to work out their personal problems through counseling and accountability. During their eight-year separation, they each experienced a lot of dying to self and re-evaluating their old ways of interrelating. Their individual changes enabled the marriage to go through a supernatural transformation. Today, they donate their time helping other couples learn what it means to be committed and transformed in a marriage.

God has planned that we would experience ongoing transformation from the time we are born again until we die and pass from kingdom life here on Earth to kingdom living in Heaven. This is called *sanctification* and it takes time! Our old ways of relating to others through our unrenewed intellect, emotions, and will are not appropriate kingdom ways. Yet God uses His Word and His Spirit to slowly see us changed into the image of His Son.

> For the word of God is living and active. Sharper than any double-edged sword, it penetrates even to dividing soul and spirit, joints and marrow; it judges the thoughts and attitudes of the heart (Hebrews 4:12 NIV).

> And we, who with unveiled faces all reflect the Lord's glory, are being transformed into his likeness with ever-increasing glory, which comes from the Lord, who is the Spirit (2 Corinthians 3:18 NIV).

> Do not conform any longer to the pattern of this world, but be transformed by the renewing of your mind. Then you will be able to test and approve what God's

will is—his good, pleasing and perfect will (Romans 12:2 NIV).

It is as we see kingdom culture revealed in Scripture that we are given a choice to either change our behavior accordingly or continue in our old way of acting and reacting. The Holy Spirit graciously works with us to convict and empower us to "put off" the old ways of worldly culture and "put on" the new ways of the kingdom of God.

God is very patient with us. He invented the process of transformation and knows it takes time. He provides plenty of instruction in His Word to help us make the necessary changes—we just have to find those instructions and follow them! For example, the Scriptures are full of "if / then" instructions from God. "If you do ____, then ____ will be the consequences." These if / then instructions can have either positive or negative consequences.

[If] "When a wise man has a controversy with a foolish man, [then] the foolish man either rages or laughs, and there is no rest" (Proverbs 29:9 NASB). *If* we have a controversy with a foolish man, *then* we will get no rest. Every parent feels this exhaustion at one time or another when they fall into the trap of arguing with their teenager! Therefore, avoid controversy with a foolish person —it's not worth it.

"Honor your father and mother (which is the first commandment with a promise), that it may be well with you, and that you may live long on the earth" (Ephesians 6:2-3 NASB). *If* we honor our parents, *then* the consequence will be long life!

If a person chooses to overuse his credit card, he will experience the consequence of debt. This is a logical consequence that God allows to happen. He doesn't usually rescue us from the consequences He has warned us about in Scripture, but instead uses them to teach us and refine us. Uncomfortable consequences force us to evaluate ourselves in the light of His Word and Spirit. In the case of an overextended credit card, we might find it helpful to study the book of Proverbs and see how we need to adjust our habits of spending.

Hopefully, we don't continue to make the same mistakes, but learn to make wise choices.

God's Word is designed to be our information manual for operating in the kingdom of God. It contains all the instructions we will need to adjust to the new culture in which we will eternally be citizens. The Lord will not magically impart kingdom culture within us. He expects us to study the manual!

This is important for us to know if we are going to adjust to our new way of living. It is also necessary for us to understand if we are going to properly relate to other kingdom people. We have to study the manual to learn how to conduct ourselves, how to respond to others, and how to adjust our attitude to be like God's. All this is necessary for living Christlike lives on planet Earth, and it is imperative in preparing for eternity future.

Chapter application

1. How does living in the here and now interrelate with the concept of being an eternal person?

2. How often do you search the Scriptures to learn God's instructions for personal relationships?

3. What is one people problem you are experiencing that would cause you to seek scriptural instruction? (For example: anger, betrayal, shame, grief, loneliness, or miscommunication.)

4. What words could you look up in a Bible concordance to help you in your research?

Chapter 2

Who Am I Really?

Terry stared at the floor as she wrung another Kleenex to shreds. "I know this sounds immature, but I can't seem to get past the conflicts with my mom. Every time I am around her the arguments start up again and usually they are about really stupid things. Even though I'm a college graduate, she makes me feel like I am never good enough!"

During Terry's adolescence, her mother had constantly criticized her choices and actions. A report card with a "B" was met with a scowl and increased study hours. Leaving dishes unwashed resulted in being grounded for a week. At 21, Terry chose to marry a carpenter instead of a doctor. Her mother skipped the wedding in disapproval.

Becoming a Christian at age 20 brought some relief to the relationship. Terry felt more comfortable than ever around her mom, and she had even been able to witness to her a few times. However, the feelings of inadequacy still hung over Terry like an old umbrella.

Unfortunately, Terry transferred these feelings to other relationships where authority figures were involved. She tended to hold herself to a very high performance standard at work and in ministry at church. She felt intense rejection when confronted by her husband, her boss, or one of the church leaders. Even her relationship with the Lord was troubling, as Terry could never feel good enough to be loved by God. Terry was caught in a web of viewing herself according to old perceptions and it was influencing her most important relationships.

You were taught, with regard to your former way of life, to put off your old self, which is being corrupted by its deceitful desires; to be made new in the attitude of your minds; and to put on the new self, created to be like God in true righteousness and holiness (Ephesians 4:22-24 NIV).

Knowing who we are created to be eternally is basic to all interpersonal relationships, for how we interact with others flows from our own self-concept. If we view ourselves according to our old self, we will think and act in ways that portray the old self. If we truly see ourselves as the new self God is forming us into, then we will think and act accordingly. Therefore, discovering this new self is vital to our eternal relationships.

For example, if I am a person who views myself as someone who has a right to be bitter because of my past hurts, then I will relate to others out of my bitterness. But, if I am a person who views others through the Cross of Forgiveness, then bitterness is no longer a filter through which I process my relationships.

Another example is the man who interacts with others based on his own insecurities and fear of people. This filter translates into relationship problems that dictate how that man will react and treat others. Shyness or, to the other extreme, manipulation and control, are often the result. However, the person who has found his identity and security in his relationship with Christ Jesus doesn't worry about what others think of him. He knows he is fully accepted and loved by the One who really matters. He can therefore freely relate to others without fear of rejection.

Eternal foundations

Insecurity and rejection are feelings common to all mankind. In fact, all are born with these feelings because all of us have come into this world with a sin nature. It is through Adam's fall that we are each born apart from God and automatically sense that separation and rejection. We immediately begin to search for a substitute that will fill the aching need within for worth and value.

Throughout our life, Satan finds opportunities to reinforce and confirm our sense of rejection and worthlessness. It is only when we are born again into a new nature that we can know true acceptance and significance. That is because we take on a new identity—that of Christ Jesus. No longer are we separated and rejected by God.

> For all have sinned and fall short of the glory of God (Romans 3:23 NIV).

> For if, by the trespass of the one man, death reigned through that one man, how much more will those who receive God's abundant provision of grace and of the gift of righteousness reign in life through the one man, Jesus Christ. Consequently, just as the result of one trespass was condemnation for all men, so also the result of one act of righteousness was justification that brings life for all men. For just as through the disobedience of the one man the many were made sinners, so also through the obedience of the one man the many will be made righteous. The law was added so that the trespass might increase. But where sin increased, grace increased all the more, so that, just as sin reigned in death, so also grace might reign through righteousness to bring eternal life through Jesus Christ our Lord (Romans 5:17-21 NIV).

> Therefore if any man be in Christ, he is a new creature: old things are passed away; behold, all things are become new (2 Corinthians 5:17 KJV).

It is only as we are in Christ that our eternal identity, individual worth, and security begin to take shape. First Corinthians 1:30-31 presents the four basic foundation stones that Jesus Christ seeks to establish within us when we become new creatures in Him:

> But by His doing you are in Christ Jesus, who became to us wisdom from God, and righteousness and sanctification, and redemption, that, just as it is written, "Let him who boasts, boast in the Lord" (1 Corinthians 1:30-31 NASB).

The foundation for our eternal personality will always be found in our relationship with Jesus Christ. Wrong foundations cannot support an eternal person! God's wisdom, righteousness, sanctification, and redemption are to be the filters through which we view ourselves and through which we relate to others.

These four foundation stones are eternal within each of us. They provide the spiritual weight that holds the rest of our identity in place. Spiritual growth only happens as we build on the wisdom, righteousness, sanctification, and redemption that Christ has become within us. If we are weak in understanding and experiencing these foundations, our growth will be unstable.

One of the ways to help apply 1 Corinthians 1:30-31 to my own life has been to speak to myself according to the truth of the Scripture passage. Personalizing each of the four foundation stones reads something like this:

Jesus has been made my wisdom. I no longer have to feel dumb, stupid, or inadequate because of a lack of education, disabilities, or slow thought processes. My identity is no longer tied into these things, but into the wisdom that He has become within me and is working out through my personality as I grow in Him.

Jesus has been made my righteousness. I no longer have to feel that I am all wrong—look wrong, act wrong, and can't do things right—because He took my "wrongness" and replaced it with His "rightness." His righteousness has made me acceptable where once I was unacceptable. The indicators of wrongness that still plague me will have to bow to the truth that I now have rightness in Christ.

Jesus has been made my sanctification. I no longer have to feel unworthy or unclean. Condemnation cannot lie to me and keep me from enjoying His presence, for He has become holiness and purity within me. My self-worth is that new person hidden in Christ, not the person I used to be, nor my present failings and mistakes.

Jesus has been made my redemption. I no longer have to be held captive to hurts. My past has no authority to hold me in bondage. Things that would come against me to wound and

24

keep me prisoner have no hold on me unless I give them place. Jesus has ransomed and delivered me. Freedom and healing are His workings within me, and His purposes through me.

> And we, who with unveiled faces all reflect the Lord's glory, are being transformed into his likeness with ever-increasing glory, which comes from the Lord, who is the Spirit (2 Corinthians 3:18 NIV).

Because we are each being made into the image of Jesus Christ, He will forever be our identity. It is from Him that our eternal personality takes shape. Our personhood is hidden in Christ and the more we recognize Him as our all in all the more He reveals our true identity and personality! Only He can make each person special and unique.

Evaluating our foundation

But, how do we know if we are basing our existence on Jesus or on other things? Sometimes, we take for granted that we have His foundations solidified in our lives. The following Scriptures and questions can help us identify where we are finding our security, personal worth, and identity, and then adjust them as needed to be in Christ Jesus.

> ➤ Do not be anxious then, saying, 'What shall we eat?' or 'What shall we drink?' or 'With what shall we clothe ourselves?' For all these things the Gentiles eagerly seek; for your heavenly Father knows that you need all these things. But seek first His kingdom and His righteousness; and all these things shall be added to you (Matthew 6:31-33 NASB).

Seeking the kingdom of God, His authority and way of doing things is to be our first priority. The Father knows our needs and will add them to our life as we keep our security in Him alone. Material goods such as food, drink, and clothes are what those without God seek for their well-being. *Question: Would your identity and security be threatened if you lost all your possessions?*

> ➤ But the LORD said to Samuel, "Do not consider his appearance or his height, for I have rejected him. The

25

LORD does not look at the things man looks at. Man looks at the outward appearance, but the LORD looks at the heart" (1 Samuel 16:7 NIV).

This is the word God gave to the prophet Samuel when Samuel assumed one of David's brothers was to be the next king of Israel. Samuel thought that the brother looked kingly and believed that he was God's choice. However, God makes it very clear that, in His kingdom, outward appearances are temporal and not something He considers important. God's concern is always the heart of a person: our motives, attitudes, and intentions. *Questions: Are you more concerned about your outward appearance or your inner attitudes and motives? Which do you spend more time on? What kind of person will you be when you are old, wrinkled, feeble, and possibly left alone in a nursing home?*

➢ Some trust in chariots and some in horses, but we trust in the name of the LORD our God (Psalm 20:7 NIV).

Chariots represent affluence and horses represent power. Both are wrong when they become the foundation of our identity. Inherent in all the names of our God is the authority of the One whose name it is. Each one of God's names represents some aspect of His eternal character. I can be secure in each of those names, for they are eternal, unchanging, and powerful. *Questions: How secure would you be if you were left without possessions and had no authority in this life—much like a slave? How well do you know the various names of God? How has each become part of your security, identity, and worth over the years of your Christian journey?*

➢ For with you is the fountain of life; in your light we see light (Psalm 36:9 NIV).

God has provided many things for us to enjoy, but they are never to replace Him as our life source. When other people, education, our career, or, even ministry, become our source of identity and self-worth, then we are building on a wrong foundation. It is only in His light and revelation that we are able to receive illumination and clarity of understanding of who we are and what our eternal worth is. *Questions: What gives you the best feeling of worth and personal identity—work, family, hobbies, ministry—or just being with Jesus? How do you know?*

> ➢ It is better to trust in the LORD than to put confidence in man. It is better to trust in the LORD than to put confidence in princes (Psalm 118:8-9 NKJV).

These verses stress that our trust is to be placed in the Lord and not in people, because people do not have the ability to meet all of our expectations. *Questions: In this passage, the word "man" represents the people we consider important in our lives. The word "princes" can represent our government. Why is using these two words important to understanding where our trust is to be placed?*

> ➢ So when you give to the needy, do not announce it with trumpets, as the hypocrites do in the synagogues and on the streets, to be honored by men. I tell you the truth, they have received their reward in full. . . . And when you pray, do not be like the hypocrites, for they love to pray standing in the synagogues and on the street corners to be seen by men. I tell you the truth, they have received their reward in full. . . . And when you pray, do not keep on babbling like pagans, for they think they will be heard because of their many words. . . . When you fast, do not look somber as the hypocrites do, for they disfigure their faces to show men they are fasting. I tell you the truth, they have received their reward in full (Matthew 6:2, 5, 7, 16 NIV).

Note how wrong motives undermine religious activity in the above verses. Ministry is good and God expects us to use the spiritual gifts He gives us. But, ministry must never become the basis for our identity. *Question: How does one know when ministry has become their identity instead of their mission?*

> ➢ Do not store up for yourselves treasures on earth, where moth and rust destroy, and where thieves break in and steal. But store up for yourselves treasures in heaven, where moth and rust do not destroy, and where thieves do not break in and steal. For where your treasure is, there your heart will be also (Matthew 6:19-21 NIV).

Our heart can tell us what kind of foundation we have in our lives, for our heart dwells in the same place that our treasure dwells. Find the priority of your heart and you will know the foundation for your personal identity. *Question: What do you find as your heart's treasure?*

> ➢ Each one should test his own actions. Then he can take pride in himself, without comparing himself to somebody else (Galatians 6:4 NIV).

We must never determine our personal worth, identity, or security by comparing ourselves with another person. Each of us must be individually established in Christ's work in us and not in what God is doing in others. Only we personally can know how far the Lord has brought us. We can evaluate our own growth, gain confidence, and boast in what God has done in us and through us. We also know areas in ourselves that may look messy right now because God is in the midst of construction in that area—and construction sites are always messy! *Question: How often do you evaluate yourself by comparing yourself with others?*

Our relationships should display the fruit of a personal identity firmly established in Christ. On the other hand, if we find that other things are dictating our sense of security, value, or worth then it is time to firm up our foundations. In the next chapter, we look at how this is done.

Chapter application

1. How would you recognize if one of the four foundations in Christ, given in 1 Corinthians 1:30-31, is missing from someone's self-concept and identity?

2. Are you personally lacking familiarity and experience with any of these four foundations?

3. What did you discover about yourself from reading the section on *Evaluating our foundations*?

Chapter 3

Adjusting My Focus

Sitting in jail was not how Joel had anticipated ending his marriage. What had started out happily ever after had ended up in divorce and a four-year jail term. Sexually abusing his stepdaughters had been a bad idea.

During this forced confinement, Joel began to think about his life choices. He read the Bible and sought answers to his sexual addictions. A process of healing began as he made Jesus Christ his Lord and began a Bible study for new believers. After his release, he found a church and a wonderful Christian woman who loved him. Today, he is a worship leader in that church and the proud father of a son.

Joel had to make major readjustments in his view of himself. Condemnation played a big part in his early Christian walk. Over time, Joel began to see himself as God saw him—a person of enormous value and worth. Slowly, his past stopped dictating his thoughts and his personal identity began to be shaped by his new understanding of who he was in Christ. Joel had to adjust his focus of attention from the facts of his past to the truth of what God was now stating about him.

All of us are like Joel in some regard. Our past can haunt us and influence our self-perception. However, transformation can begin once we have recognized areas where we are lacking Jesus Christ as the foundation for our security, worth, and identity. Once we know how God views us, we can refuse to give attention to the facts about our old self. Truth can be emphasized over facts and a new belief system formed concerning our new self.

A woman may focus her attention on the fact that she has had an abortion and may feel dirty or unworthy because of that fact. God, however, would have her focus on the truth that she has been forgiven and stands sinless before Him. So often we get caught up in the facts about ourselves rather than the truth that God has declared about us.

If we focus our attention on the facts about our life rather than God's truth concerning us, then we begin to believe the facts rather than the truth! This is not to say that we deny the facts. The facts have to be clearly acknowledged and confessed if sin is involved before truth can take the place of them. However, there has to come a time when we begin to concentrate on God's truth concerning our facts.

God often has to change our focus from self-centered to God-centered before He can work in us and utilize us in His service. Moses was a terrific example of this. The Lord had great plans for Moses, but God first had to humble him. So God sent Moses into the wilderness for forty years to tend sheep. The cocky attitude that had once caused Moses to take matters into his own hands was definitely knocked out of him during that time!

In fact, the opposite extreme in pride became Moses' new problem. He developed a very low self-image. In both extremes, he was focusing on himself. Moses needed to acquire his self-identity from his relationship with the Lord and not from his life circumstances or his mistakes.

Anointing and authority flow out of our personal identity in Christ Jesus. This was something that Moses learned the hard way. We find his story in Exodus, chapters three and four. The following narrative describes how he lost part of his anointing and authority because he focused on facts rather than on the truth of who he was to be in God. The account begins with Moses tending his father-in-law's sheep:

> Now Moses was tending the flock of Jethro his father-in-law, the priest of Midian, and he led the flock to the far side of the desert and came to Horeb, the mountain

of God. There the angel of the LORD appeared to him in flames of fire from within a bush. Moses saw that though the bush was on fire it did not burn up. So Moses thought, "I will go over and see this strange sight—why the bush does not burn up."

When the LORD saw that he had gone over to look, God called to him from within the bush, "Moses! Moses!" And Moses said, "Here I am."

"Do not come any closer," God said. "Take off your sandals, for the place where you are standing is holy ground." Then he said, "I am the God of your father, the God of Abraham, the God of Isaac and the God of Jacob." At this, Moses hid his face, because he was afraid to look at God. The LORD said, "I have indeed seen the misery of my people in Egypt. I have heard them crying out because of their slave drivers, and I am concerned about their suffering. So I have come down to rescue them from the hand of the Egyptians and to bring them up out of that land into a good and spacious land, a land flowing with milk and honey— the home of the Canaanites, Hittites, Amorites, Perizzites, Hivites and Jebusites. And now the cry of the Israelites has reached me, and I have seen the way the Egyptians are oppressing them. So now, go. I am sending you to Pharaoh to bring my people the Israelites out of Egypt" (Exodus 3:1-10 NIV).

Now note the excuse Moses gave in response to God's call. It could almost sound humble:

But Moses said to God, "Who am I, that I should go to Pharaoh and bring the Israelites out of Egypt?" (Exodus 3:11 NIV).

True humility, however, focuses on God. Moses was focused on self and was responding out of inferiority rather than confidence in what he was called to be in God.

God responded by reassuring Moses that He would be with him. He promised to bring Moses back to the place where they were

31

meeting to validate the work to which God was calling him. God was trying to refocus Moses' attention!

> And God said, "I will be with you. And this will be the sign to you that it is I who have sent you: When you have brought the people out of Egypt, you will worship God on this mountain" (Exodus 3:12 NIV).

Despite all this, Moses was still focused on himself and his inadequacies. His questions indicated his insecurities:

> Moses said to God, "Suppose I go to the Israelites and say to them, 'The God of your fathers has sent me to you,' and they ask me, 'What is his name?' Then what shall I tell them?" (Exodus 3:13 NIV).

A more specific response flowed from God as He (again) tried to get Moses to refocus his attention. He declared His name as "I Am Who I Am," told Moses to go to the elders, and gave Moses a specific message. God was declaring truth against the facts that Moses was presenting.

Moses still continued to give excuses, shifting his attention from what God was declaring to his own fears:

> Moses answered, "What if they do not believe me or listen to me and say, 'The LORD did not appear to you'?" (Exodus 4:1 NIV).

The Lord had totally thought out the whole program of deliverance for Israel and nothing was going to take Him by surprise or catch Him unprepared. Moses, however, had a hard time believing that! His insecurity was based on his limited view of himself and of the Lord. God took one more step to perform signs and wonders designed to refocus Moses' attention back to truth:

> Then the LORD said to him, "What is that in your hand?" "A staff," he replied. The LORD said, "Throw it on the ground." Moses threw it on the ground and it became a snake, and he ran from it. Then the LORD said to him, "Reach out your hand and take it by the tail." So Moses reached out and took hold of the snake and it turned back into a staff in his hand. "This," said

the LORD, "is so that they may believe that the LORD, the God of their fathers—the God of Abraham, the God of Isaac and the God of Jacob—has appeared to you."

Then the LORD said, "Put your hand inside your cloak." So Moses put his hand into his cloak, and when he took it out, it was leprous, like snow. "Now put it back into your cloak," he said. So Moses put his hand back into his cloak, and when he took it out, it was restored, like the rest of his flesh. Then the LORD said, "If they do not believe you or pay attention to the first miraculous sign, they may believe the second. But if they do not believe these two signs or listen to you, take some water from the Nile and pour it on the dry ground. The water you take from the river will become blood on the ground" (Exodus 4:2-9 NIV).

At this point, Moses shifted gears by bringing up the fact of his poor communication skills. God again answered him patiently and with truth:

Moses said to the LORD, "O Lord, I have never been eloquent, neither in the past nor since you have spoken to your servant. I am slow of speech and tongue." The LORD said to him, "Who gave man his mouth? Who makes him deaf or mute? Who gives him sight or makes him blind? Is it not I, the LORD? Now go; I will help you speak and will teach you what to say" (Exodus 4:10-12 NIV).

Finally the root problem came out. Moses didn't want to go and all his excuses were just that—excuses!

But Moses said, "O Lord, please send someone else to do it" (Exodus 4:13 NIV).

God's frustration was finally revealed, and He wouldn't take no for an answer.

Then the LORD'S anger burned against Moses and he said, "What about your brother, Aaron the Levite? I know he can speak well. He is already on his way to meet you, and his heart will be glad when he sees you. You shall speak to him and put words in his mouth; I will help both of you speak and will teach you what to do. He will speak to the people for you, and it will be as if he were your mouth and as if you were God to him. But take this staff in your hand so you can perform miraculous signs with it" (Exodus 4:14-17 NIV).

The experience at the burning bush was to mark Moses' life. At times, he was able to be all that God declared him to be. At other times, he failed to focus on God and his self-focus greatly cost both him and the nation of Israel. Like Moses, our eternal identities will take a lifetime to develop. But as we learn to acknowledge facts and keep our focus of attention on truth, we will find ourselves walking in security and worth as well as anointing.

Because we gravitate toward the focus of our attention, we often end up seeing ourselves as less than how God sees us. To a great degree, we determine the type of identity we will have depending on what is the focus of our attention. If we do not see ourselves as God sees us, then we won't believe the things He tells us! The purpose of the following chart is to demonstrate that many believers subconsciously dwell on facts rather than truth. If it is usually *facts* that get your attention in your thought life and words, then you need to refocus on *truth*. Begin giving yourself pep talks according to scriptural truth. Refuse to think according to the facts.

Fact: People don't like me.

Truth: God has freely bestowed His grace upon me and He has already adopted me into His family. It doesn't matter what others think of me because the One who matters most thinks I am so wonderful that He has made me His own child (based on Ephesians 1:6).

Fact: I don't feel forgiven for past sins.

Truth: God has reconciled me through Christ's death so that I might be presented as holy in His sight. I am without blemish and I am free from accusation. It doesn't matter what I feel, for the truth is that I am forgiven (based on Colossians 1:22).

Fact: Others are so much more spiritual than me.

Truth: I am confident of this, that He who has begun a good work in me will carry it on to completion until the day of Christ Jesus. My spiritual development is not based on how spiritual others are; it is rooted in what Christ has begun in me and is continuing to do in me (based on Philippians 1:6).

Fact: I don't feel like I fit anywhere. I don't feel like I belong.

Truth: All believers have been given the Holy Spirit and baptized by Him into one body—myself included. God has placed and arranged all the parts of this body just as He wanted them to be. I do belong and I do fit. God has a special place just for me (based on 1 Corinthians 12:13, 18).

Fact: I'm not an attractive looking person.

Truth: The Lord has given me a crown of beauty, the oil of gladness, and a garment of praise. These are the things that make me attractive to Him and to others. I will be called an oak of righteousness, a planting of the Lord for the display of His splendor. He thinks that I am so attractive that He is displaying me as an object of splendor (based on Isaiah 61:3).

Fact: I can't read well and am a slow learner.

Truth: God's Word is perfect and it will make "simple me" wise! The unfolding of Scripture gives me understanding beyond that of other book learning. As I read, memorize, and meditate on His Word, then I will find that I am a wise person, regardless of my IQ or learning disabilities (based on Psalm 19:7 and 119:130).

Fact: My mate has no desire to change from his or her ways to God's ways.

Truth: Jesus said that if I rely on my mate to change then it won't happen. I have to rely on God to bring change to my mate. In fact, the Lord is more committed to my mate changing than I am and nothing is impossible with God (based on Matthew 19:26).

Chapter application

1. Design your own chart like the one above. What are some facts that you believe about yourself that should be changed? What Scriptures will you use to refocus your attention onto truth? Write those Scriptures out, begin to memorize them, and speak them to yourself on a daily basis.

2. What are some practical ways that a believer can put off the old self listed under *facts* and begin to put on the new self listed under *truth* in the chart?

3. Obviously, the principle of changing our focus applies to how we view others also. What do you really believe about the people you relate to, and why do you believe the things you do about them? Do you tend to see negative facts about others, or do you focus on God's truth about others as found in His Scriptures?

Chapter 4

Getting Real

Eagerly extending my hand, I greeted Pat. I was surprised to see her shopping at Kmart, as she had lived in another community now for quite some time. Apparently, she was visiting her mom for a few weeks. It was good to see her. She had been a part of our church for several years.

After catching up on all the news about our children, I expressed how happy everyone would be to see her if she had time to come to church during her visit. Pat looked surprised and explained that she really didn't plan to attend our church. She felt that my husband, the elders, and myself were not good church leaders.

Taken aback, I tried to keep smiling as I quickly asked the Holy Spirit to help me wisely respond. Pat casually explained that she would be attending another church in the city and just wanted to be honest about her feelings. She "wouldn't be a good Christian if she didn't tell me the truth." I managed to express my regret that she felt that way and that she would always be welcome to come and visit old friends. Having expressed herself honestly, she excused herself and continued with her shopping.

Watching her walk off in her hippy clothes, I realized that she had articulated what had become a popular theme in the 60s and 70s: To be truly authentic, you must be verbally honest about what you feel and think. However, that philosophy is not kingdom philosophy. God wants us to speak truth, but it must be His truth and it must be cushioned in love.

37

But speaking the truth in love, we are to grow up in all [aspects] into Him, who is the head, [even] Christ (Ephesians 4:15 NASB).

Now that you have purified yourselves by obeying the truth so that you have sincere love for your brothers, love one another deeply, from the heart (1 Peter 1:22 NIV).

Bleeding love

Around 1,000 years ago, Viking Leif Ericson landed on the east coast of North America and began a colony called Vineland. Although the Vikings were fierce warriors, they had a difficult time with the Native Americans. The Vikings were confused by the Indians and believed that they were often demons in disguise. The problem of distinguishing a real Indian from a demon was simple: Authenticity was established by blood. A real Indian would bleed when stabbed while a demon would disappear.

We can verify a Christian with a similar test of authenticity. When a Christian is "stabbed," he bleeds love. This is especially true when wounded by other believers. "A new command I give you: Love one another. As I have loved you, so you must love one another. By this all men will know that you are my disciples, if you love one another" (John 13:34-35 NIV).

Love is the core of Christianity. Everything we do must represent the love demonstrated by God towards us. This means that we should be genuine in our relationships. No masks, facades, or pretenses. We are to be authentic with each other. Authenticity contains the idea of humility and honesty in how we present ourselves and how we respond to others. We are to be people experiencing the ongoing transformation of God's Spirit, Word, and truth conforming us into His image.

Authenticity, however, is not necessarily the open sharing of our feelings. Our feelings are sometimes wrong. Feelings that reflect our sin nature need to be adjusted rather than fully expressed. Just because I am feeling angry does not give me the right to lose my temper with my family. Kingdom culture states that I am to let peace rule in my heart and remove anger from my speaking (see Colossians 3:15, Ephesians 4:31, and Colossians 3:8). Let is a powerful word and means that I have the ability to choose a peaceful heart and a calm voice in place of turmoil within and a loud, angry tone of voice.

Joe and Tina were in counseling regarding their communication problems and anger issues. As we reviewed the Scriptures mentioned above, Joe suggested a statement that would indicate the need for a time out whenever their arguments began to escalate to the point of hurtful words. "I'm feeling really angry right now and am trying to replace it with peace," became their signal to back off from the argument and give each other time to prepare their heart and words to reflect those of Jesus.

Although that statement might sound odd to us, it worked for Joe and Tina. It is a scriptural comment that conveys a wrong emotion without approving of it. It is honest, yet humble, and it accepts responsibility for change. Further authenticity for Joe and Tina meant that they were to stop any action that was expressing unrighteous anger and were to replace it with an action that promoted peace. Sometimes this meant just leaving the room.

As believers, we should not tell our spouse that we do not love him or her even though that might seem true at the moment. However true it might feel, it would be unkind, and kindness is a kingdom law (see Proverbs 31:26). The authentic statement is to say, "I am learning to love you as Christ loved the Church." Such a statement communicates truth and an ownership of the need to grow and develop in everything that love represents.

Real vulnerability

It is also authentic to communicate our weaknesses and need for help. Galatians 6:2 states, "Carry each other's burdens, and in this way you will fulfill the law of Christ" (NIV). In order to have another help carry our burdens, we must communicate what our burdens are! The same is true with sin. "Therefore confess your sins to each other and pray for each other so that you may be healed" (James 5:16 NIV). Kingdom people aren't afraid to make their weaknesses or sins known.

The apostle Paul did not hesitate to make his blemishes public knowledge. In fact, he even went so far as to boast about his limitations! It was through frailty that Paul learned to tap into the awesome power of Almighty God. It was through his weaknesses that people were able to see the power of God dwelling in Paul. "And He has said to me, 'My grace is sufficient for you, for power is perfected in weakness.' Most gladly, therefore, I will rather boast about my weaknesses, that the power of Christ may dwell in me" (2 Corinthians 12:9 NASB).

Confessing sins and weaknesses to others is not regarded as noble in the culture of the world. Many regard the person who does so as flawed. It is amazing to me how much we hide our sins and weaknesses. I have encountered this inconsistency in Christian homes and in church leadership, where the philosophy is often to appear that we have our act so together that there is nothing to confess, no weakness to acknowledge. Vulnerability is avoided at all costs. Nevertheless, it is in the leadership of our churches and homes that vulnerability is to be modeled for the rest of us.

When we neglect to make ourselves vulnerable to others, we project the image that we are strong and capable. We appear so spiritually mature that we have no need for God or others. That type of thinking is directly opposed to kingdom authenticity! Paul was one of the most spiritual of men, yet he continually exposed his sins and weaknesses. Two thousand years later, we are still gleaning from his wisdom, anointing, and authority because he was willing to be authentic. How many of us would write down our sins and limitations for people to read about for ages to come?

Unfortunately, it is common for believers to continue to act and react according to their old ways of relating to others. Often, we assume that our words and actions are a genuine representation of truth. It takes time for us to learn that kingdom culture requires different responses than the culture of this world. A soft answer to turn away wrath may not seem logical to us, nor does dealing with our anger before sundown seem reasonable when we are used to indulging our hostility for several days.

Confessing our weaknesses and sins definitely goes against the world culture! As believers, our actions and responses must be biblically based rather than feeling-centered. That is true kingdom authenticity.

Becoming biblically centered

Nehemiah 8:8-12 records the grief of the Israeli people after returning from captivity and hearing the Scriptures read to them by Ezra the priest. Weeping seemed a logical response given the solemn occasion of the Feast of Trumpets, because the people realized how they had neglected to obey the Law of the Lord. However, the leaders felt that sorrow was an inappropriate response and that the people should instead rejoice at the reading. They commanded the people to do things that would bring joy—feast and celebrate. The correct expression of joy was not the inclination of the crowd, but it was the authentic expression that was due the reading of the Law at that time.

> They read from the Book of the Law of God, making it clear and giving the meaning so that the people could understand what was being read. Then Nehemiah the governor, Ezra the priest and scribe, and the Levites who were instructing the people said to them all, "This day is sacred to the LORD your God. Do not mourn or weep." For all the people had been weeping as they listened to the words of the Law. Nehemiah said, "Go and enjoy choice food and sweet drinks, and send some to those who have nothing prepared. This day is sacred to our Lord. Do not grieve, for the joy of the LORD is your strength." The Levites calmed all the people, saying, "Be still, for this is a sacred day. Do not grieve." Then all the people went away to eat and drink, to send portions of food and to celebrate with great joy, because they now understood the words that had been made known to them (Nehemiah 8:8-12 NIV).

Faith sometimes means doing the exact opposite of what you feel. Ted Roberts has said, "It is always easier to act yourself into a feeling then to feel yourself into an action." Therefore, authenticity is not necessarily expressing our feelings, but

41

expressing what God considers correct responses to situations. Correct feelings will follow correct actions, just as the action of feasting and celebrating brought the correct feelings of joy rather than grief to the people of Israel.

True authenticity will require that we know God's Word and its instructions so that we can respond rightly in any given situation. Most of this book is dedicated to showing the correct scriptural actions and responses to various situations. Learn them, practice them, and mentor others in them, and you will find yourself walking in authentic kingdom culture.

> Pay attention and listen to the sayings of the wise; apply your heart to what I teach, for it is pleasing when you keep them in your heart and have all of them ready on your lips. So that your trust may be in the LORD, I teach you today, even you. Have I not written thirty sayings for you, sayings of counsel and knowledge, teaching you true and reliable words, so that you can give sound answers to him who sent you? (Proverbs 22:17-21 NIV).

Eternal consequences

Seeking to accurately represent the Lord Jesus has eternal consequences. Those who look at us and see a reflection of Jesus will be drawn to His love and forgiveness. When they accept His salvation, they become eternal people along with us. Consequently, when we don't take seriously the requirement to be authentic, then we repel those whom Christ loves. A day of accountability is coming for each of us.

> But I tell you that men will have to give account on the day of judgment for every careless word they have spoken. For by your words you will be acquitted, and by your words you will be condemned (Matthew 12:36-37 NIV).

> For we must all appear before the judgment seat of Christ, that each one may receive what is due him for the things done while in the body, whether good or bad (2 Corinthians 5:10 NIV).

God considers how we treat and speak to others so important that our actions and words will be used on the Day of Judgment to condemn or acquit us. As believers, this acquittal or condemnation is not about *where* we will spend eternity. The Judgment Seat of Christ is not related to our salvation. Jesus has already paid the sin price for us to experience eternal life in His presence.

The Judgment Seat of Christ will, however, determine our eternal reward. Wrong actions and words will be used against us unless they have been dealt with through repentance and forgiveness. Right actions and words that reflect the work of Calvary will be used to vindicate us. In fact, they will determine what eternal reward we will receive from the Lord!

> Each man's work will become evident; for the day will show it, because it is [to be] revealed with fire; and the fire itself will test the quality of each man's work. If any man's work which he has built upon it remains, he shall receive a reward. If any man's work is burned up, he shall suffer loss; but he himself shall be saved, yet so as through fire (1 Corinthians 3:13-15 NASB).

The rewards spoken of in the Scriptures are referred to as crowns. Scripture mentions several different types of crowns awaiting believers. First Thessalonians 2:19-20 tells us that people are one of the crowns we will receive as an eternal reward. This particular crown is called the Crown of Exultation. "For who is our hope or joy or crown of exultation? Is it not even you, in the presence of our Lord Jesus at His coming? For you are our glory and joy" (NASB).

Isn't that interesting? People are important! How we treat each other and how we speak to one another determines if others will be a part of our Crown of Exultation. I get the impression that, when Jesus returns, we will all be reflecting what He has done in us through others, as well as reflecting His glory in how He has used us in others' lives. That reflection will be a bright, shimmering light around our heads mirroring people—our Crown of Exultation.

The testing that will determine our rewards is one of fire. The fire of the Lord will burn away all those things that are considered eternally worthless. There are those who will have everything burnt away and be left standing with only their salvation as their reward. Others will have allowed the burning process to start early in their kingdom walk and will have much more than just salvation that will survive the flames. The works that survive God's fire will be more than just good deeds. They include the godly conduct toward others that reveals a renewed mind and consecrated heart.

> I the LORD search the heart and examine the mind, to reward a man according to his conduct, according to what his deeds deserve (Jeremiah 17:10 NIV).

> Those who check into their thought life and evaluate their actions will avoid having unrighteous deeds build up in their life that eventually will be destroyed in God's inferno. By judging ourselves now, we can prevent future burnout!

> But if we judged ourselves rightly, we should not be judged. But when we are judged, we are disciplined by the Lord in order that we may not be condemned along with the world (1 Corinthians 11:31-32 NASB).

> Watch out that you do not lose what you have worked for, but that you may be rewarded fully (2 John 1:8 NIV).

To refine gold, a goldsmith must heat gold nuggets extracted from the Earth until the impurities are separated from the pure gold. It is only at the point where the goldsmith can see his reflection in the smelting pot that he knows the process is complete. Becoming an authentic kingdom person is a lifelong process that includes allowing the fire of the Holy Spirit to burn away our impurities so that the Lord will only see a reflection of Himself when He looks at us.

Chapter application

1. Explain the difference between kingdom authenticity and what our culture teaches about being authentic.

2. Describe one thing you can begin to do to become more biblically authentic in your relationships.

3. Briefly describe how you can actively judge yourself so that combustible things can be removed from your life now rather than at the Judgment Seat of Christ.

Part Two

It's All About Them!

Chapter 5

Ouch—That Hurt!

Tom and I had been involved in ministry only a few years when I experienced the betrayal of a friend from church. "You know I wouldn't say this if I didn't love you," was her introduction to a very destructive avalanche of criticism. It came as quite a shock, as I had naively believed that Christians didn't do this type of thing. Hurt beyond understanding, I pulled away from people and hibernated within the confines of just motherhood duties. L.I.F.E. Bible College had not prepared me for this type of wound. Confused, I began to search the Scriptures for instructions on how I was supposed to process this pain. There had to be answers somewhere within the pages of the 66 books of the Bible.

Slowly, over nine months, my notebooks were filled with Scripture passages related to offense. I began to experience healing as God's Word was applied. I learned more in the process than I had bargained for, as God wanted to address further arenas than just my hurt feelings. Categories emerged that addressed all aspects of offense. This chapter and the next are the result of those nine months of study. Of course, it is taking years for me to actually put all this stuff into practice, but the results in my relationships have been well worth the effort.

All of us have had our feelings hurt at some point or another. Even Paul and Barnabas had their very verbal disagreements in the midst of missionary service, so we are in good company. In the book of Acts, the first deacon board was formed for the specific purpose of dealing with a group of widows who were offended because their needs weren't being met by the church. So, hurt feelings, disagreements, and people getting upset have been a part of church life for a very long time! First Corinthians 11:17-19 addresses this problem.

> But in giving this instruction, I do not praise you, because you come together not for the better but for the worse. For, in the first place, when you come together as a church, I hear that divisions exist among you; and in part, I believe it. For there must also be factions among you, in order that those who are approved may have become evident among you (NASB).

God allows disunity and division among His people so that it will reveal those who know how to rightly process conflict and those who don't! People who handle offenses with scriptural integrity are those who are more qualified and approved for leadership in the kingdom of God. Leaders will be recognized by their ability to wisely handle disagreements and strife in their own relationships, as well as in the corporate body. Few churches follow this process for evaluating possible leadership, but it is one of the main qualifiers set down in the Word of God. Understanding how to deal with offense is crucial to all mature relationships in the kingdom.

The Scriptures use several different words for our one word, *offense*. Each paints a word picture to help us better understand the meaning of offense. In the Old Testament two Hebrew words are used: (1) *Mikshoh* means "a stumbling block" or "to fall." This is a true description of offense because a person always stumbles within before he stumbles in his outward reactions. This is why we often refer to offense as hurt *feelings*. (2) *Pasha* means "to break away from just authority" or "to trespass." Unfortunately, offense often happens when we overstep our boundaries or trespass on another's personal boundaries. Clearly, rebellion has offense at its core.

In the New Testament, the Greek word *skandalizo* is used and means to "entrap, trip up, to stumble and entice to sin." It is from *skandalizo* that our English word *scandal* originates.

Offense is a trap: once caught up in it, one finds it hard to untangle the resulting mess. In addition, offense is often the welcome mat to all sorts of temptations in life.

Offense lies at the root of most interpersonal relationship problems, both with others and with God. It was the first reaction of Satan as he initiated and nurtured pride in his heart. It led to his rebellion against the Lord and God's subsequent rejection and condemnation of him. Offense is the explanation for the old sin nature operating in our lives and often the reason we fail to walk in the power of the Holy Spirit. It is usually the first door Satan uses to bringing temptations into someone's life.

In counseling, offense is frequently at the end of the trail we follow in a person's life to find the origin of a problem. Some sort of offense is consistently the initial cause of anger, rebellion, hurt feelings, shame, pride, depression, and adultery, whether the offense is against a person or against God and His ways. Sometimes we are the cause of offense; other times, we are the victims of another's offense. Even when we are the victims of offense, we still tend to take offense and give offense. If we can understand how offense works and how to deal with it on a personal level, then we can avoid personal sin and wounds.

Two commands

First Peter 2:5 calls each of us to be living stones. "You also, like living stones, are being built into a spiritual house to be a holy priesthood, offering spiritual sacrifices acceptable to God through Jesus Christ" (NIV). Stones come in all shapes and sizes, and a master mason will fit them together in such a way that function and beauty are the final results of a building. Often stones must be reshaped to fit with other stones. The stones really don't have much input on where they are to be fitted. Their responsibility is simply to be available to be chipped and placed in the structure according to the mason's design.

As our Master Mason, God works with us as living stones. This implies that we have more of a part to play than regular, *dead* stones that are used as building materials. We have to be willing to be chipped and reshaped according to our Mason's design for the spiritual house He is building. Living stones can always walk off the construction project if they so desire. Some people do so because they don't like the other stones that God wants to fit around them. In addition, many of us don't like the idea that it is often other people that God uses to rub the sharp points off our personality as He reshapes us for His purposes. Therefore, becoming a "spiritual house" involves commitment to God's project and commitment to our relationships with other believers.

Offense will destroy a spiritual building project faster than any other form of destruction. Knowing this, God gives us two commands to keep His house design intact. The first command is found in 1 Corinthians 10:32: "Give no offense either to Jews or to Greeks or to the church of God" (NASB). This is a simple command—don't offend anyone. The second command is found in Philippians 1:10: "That you may approve the things that are excellent, that you may be sincere and without offense till the day of Christ" (NKJV). This also is a simple command—don't get offended.

Two simple commands that are almost impossible to obey! We aren't allowed to give offense or to be offended, yet God wouldn't have said these things if they were unattainable. Everything that we need to know about handling offense can be learned as we evaluate our lives and look to the Scriptures. Once we know some of the danger areas and signs of offense, we can search the Scriptures for God's how-to instructions concerning offense, and follow them.

"Danger, Do Not Enter"

All of us have areas in our lives where we can easily be offended or can easily give offense. These are the arenas where we must be on the alert for offense to happen. One such arena is the area of *unmet expectations*. Usually, it is a lack of communication that lies at the bottom of unmet expectations.

Mary found herself getting very offended with her husband when they were first married because he never took out the garbage. In her family, it was always the men who took out the garbage. She didn't know that in his family it had always been the women. Mary had an unmet expectation based on her own unspoken rule.

I recently talked with a pastor who was offended because his elders were not doing things the way the pastor expected and appeared to be overstepping their authority. I asked him if he had given his elders a job description and he replied that he had not. Since boundary lines had not been clearly defined, people were unknowingly causing offense. This was his fault, not theirs. His frustrations could have been avoided through proper communication and clearly defined expectations. This would also have allowed the elders to think through their own expectations before discussion of any discrepancies with the pastor.

Confrontation is another danger area for offense. No one likes to be confronted and most of us don't like to confront others. However, confrontation is a part of life. Love confronts. God confronted us when He gave us the Ten Commandments. Confrontation has to be done if people are to grow. *How* it is done is what determines if offense or growth results. If we know that confrontation is an area where offense can occur, then we need to evaluate the way we confront others and how we receive confrontation.

The avalanche of criticism mentioned at the beginning of this chapter might have gone much differently if my friend had approached me with a less self-righteous attitude. While her comments contained some truths, they were missed because of her cutting words. A few compliments thrown in could have softened the blow and allowed me to evaluate her observations. I needed to know that, behind her confrontation, was a heart that was *for* me and not against me.

Assumption can also be a danger area for most of us. Sally had been sick for a number of years with an undefined illness. Her friend, Jean, confidently expressed her belief that Sally's illness was directly related to a dietary fast Sally had been following. Jean felt the fast was undermining Sally's health. What Jean did not know was that the fast was only a few weeks long and that it had been completed. The type of fast Sally had chosen had been through a doctor's recommendation. Jean ended up looking rather foolish because she had not researched her facts before she gave her opinion. She assumed something that was not true. Sally ended up feeling offended and under Jean's judgment.

Often, we fail to get the facts of a situation and we assume something that may not be true. We infer things that are not there. Poor decisions based on assumption are often the result. I have friends who left their church because they assumed that no one there liked them. Others have assumed negative things about a person without hearing the person's full story. We must be careful not to be offended about something for which we do not have all the information.

A final danger area worth mentioning is the time when our bodies are experiencing a hormonal or chemical imbalance. Many people suffer a chemical imbalance when their serotonin levels are depleted, usually a result of stress. A woman's monthly cycle can bring on hormonal imbalances that create an atmosphere for offense for her and for all those around her. Because this is an occasional danger area for me, I have learned to give myself pep talks before I go out in public. At least once a month on a Sunday morning I will lecture myself before service, "Susan, don't talk about anything serious with anyone. Smile, nod and be silent."

Sometimes we are oblivious to the fact that we have become offended. One of the indications that we have just entered a "Danger, Do Not Enter" area of offense can be a feeling of irritation. Frustration is often a signal that we are getting offended. Defensiveness is another caution, because if our thought life is in a defensive mode, then we are probably offended. Putting up walls in a relationship or distancing oneself from family, friends, and church activities is another warning sign.

The problem of offense is only going to increase as the end times approach. Years ago, Campbell McAlpine was teaching on offense at our church and explained how Matthew 24:10 was written to believers concerning the end times: "And then shall many be offended, and shall betray one another, and shall hate one another" (KJV). Note the progression in this verse: offense leads to betrayal, which leads to hatred. Because of this pattern, Campbell stated that, "Every offended Christian is a potential betrayer."

Satan's strategy is always to divide and conquer the relationships of believers through offense. Luke writes of Paul's encounters with offense and betrayal in Acts 24 and includes Paul's statement in verse 16, "This being so, I myself always strive to have a conscience without offense toward God and men" (NKJV). May this be our commitment also: to have a conscience that is free of offense.

Three preventative measures for offense

People plan weddings, vacations, and retirement. However, no one wakes up in the morning with the thought, "I think I'll get offended today." We don't intend for offense to happen. Unfortunately, neither do we take precautions to avoid offense. It just happens! Yet, the Scriptures give three different ingredients as preventative measures in our lives for offense: (1) God's Word, (2) a renewed mind, and (3) the use of prudence, knowledge, and discernment.

Psalm 119:165 states, "Great peace have they which love thy law: and nothing shall offend them" (KJV). This Scripture contains both a promise and a condition. It is one of those "if _____, then _____" verses discussed in Chapter One. If I love God's Word (the condition), then nothing will be able to offend me (the promise)! How does this work?

The more we get God's Word into our mind and heart, the more peace reigns in our lives. Things that used to offend us no longer are an issue. God's Word has become the deciding force of our personal identity, not what others say or think about us. We have to allow His Word, also called a two-edged sword, to work as a scalpel within our attitudes and motives, cutting off all patterns of thinking that are different than what Scripture declares. This is how we become conformed into His image.

In John 16:1 Jesus states it this way, "These things have I spoken unto you, that ye should not be offended" (KJV). Jesus said many things during His life here on Earth. However, the totality of Scripture also represents Christ because one of His names is Word of God (see Revelation 19:13). He intentionally told us many things so that we would listen, follow His instructions, and not become offended.

The Scriptures are to act like positive pressure within our personalities, resisting any other pressure coming against us. A balloon will stay blown up as long as the pressure inside the balloon is greater than the pressure pushing against it from its surface. If the outside pressure becomes greater than the pressure within, the balloon will pop. In the same way, God's Word is to become a positive force within us. As long as this pressure is greater than any stress we are experiencing from without, we won't cave in.

Knowing God's Word involves more than just reading the Bible. We have to practice what we learn from our study of the Scriptures. Hebrews 5:11-14 further identifies the practice of God's Word as the agent that will enable us to discern good from evil.

> We have much to say about this, but it is hard to explain because you are slow to learn. In fact, though by this time you ought to be teachers, you need someone to teach you the elementary truths of God's word all over again. You need milk, not solid food! Anyone who lives on milk, being still an infant, is not acquainted with the teaching about righteousness. But solid food is for the mature, who by constant use have trained themselves to distinguish good from evil (NIV).

An example of practicing God's Word on a constant basis would be to carefully study the Scriptures contained in this chapter and the next. Then, whenever you have an opportunity to be offended, make a decision to respond according to the instruction of these Scriptures, rather than how you might have reacted in the past. Over time, you will find maturity happening in your life as you continue to put these Scriptures into practice.

You will also find that you are able to distinguish good and evil in your actions and reactions with others. You will know when you are reacting in a way contrary to God's way when you encounter an offense, and you will know when you have responded in a good way. The evil motives or misunderstood good motives of others will be much easier to discern as you continue to actively respond to offenses according to scriptural instruction.

The second preventative measure for offense is the renewing of your mind. Your mind did not become saved along with your spirit; it still thinks and processes things according to old habit patterns. Romans 12:2 states that our minds have to be transformed in order to discern God's will in various situations. "Do not conform any longer to the pattern of this world, but be transformed by the renewing of your mind. Then you will be able to test and approve what God's will is—his good, pleasing and perfect will" (NIV). Transformation happens the more our minds are renewed to think the way God thinks.

It is within our old thinking patterns that Satan uses his tricks to rope us into offense. Second Corinthians 2:11 advises us to be aware of this danger. "Lest Satan should take advantage of us; for we are not ignorant of his devices" (NKJV). The word *devices* in this verse is better translated from the Greek as *mind devices*. Any area of our mind that is not renewed to God's way of thinking is a place where Satan can influence us. Second Corinthians 10:3-5 provides directions on how to renew our minds:

> For though we walk in the flesh, we do not war after the flesh: (For the weapons of our warfare are not carnal, but mighty through God to the pulling down of strong holds;) Casting down imaginations, and every high thing that exalteth itself against the knowledge of God, and bringing into captivity every thought to the obedience of Christ (KJV).

This will not be easy! You must be committed to doing the following:

1. Tune into your reactions to people and situations. Ask yourself, "What am I feeling, and why am I feeling this way?"

2. Listen to your self-talk. What is the inner conversation going on in your mind? Does it sound like the peace of God type of talk or is it more along the lines of defensiveness and frustration?

3. After you have tuned into your thoughts and feelings, try to identify the wrong reasoning and thought patterns that are contrary to scriptural ways of reasoning.

4. Once you have identified the thinking that is exalting itself above the way that God would have you think, simply refuse to listen to these wrong ways of thinking.

5. Replace these wrong ways of thinking with the Scriptures from this chapter and the next concerning God's ways of processing offense.

6. Act out the instructions of these Scriptures. Do what the Word says! Refuse to do things the way you have in the past! Only then will you find maturity happening in your life, and only then will you be on the preventative side of offense!

The third preventative measure for offense is to move in knowledge, prudence, and discernment whenever we encounter an occasion for offense. Prudence is the ability to look right through a situation and see both sides of it at the same time. Someone has said that it is insight that draws a godly conclusion. Philippians 1:9-10 states, "And this I pray, that your love may abound yet more and more in *knowledge and in all judgment;* That ye may approve things that are excellent; *that ye may be sincere and without offense till the day of Christ*" (KJV, *italics mine*).

The ability to move in this type of discernment and wisdom is a direct result of practicing the first two preventative measures. Once you have begun to act on God's Word that you have put into your heart and mind, and have begun to see your mind renewed, then prudence and discernment will accompany your relationships.

A good example of knowledge, prudence, and discernment is Solomon's comment in Ecclesiastes 7:21-22. "Do not pay attention to every word people say, or you may hear your servant cursing you—for you know in your heart that many times you yourself have cursed others" (NIV). This is one Scripture we should all memorize and practice!

Chapter application

1. What are some of your personal danger areas for offense?

2. Matthew 24:10 is a warning given to believers during the end times. How have you seen this pattern of division happen in your own life, in your family, in the life of other friends, or in a church?

3. In your opinion, what part does criticism play in the Matthew 24:10 pattern? How does James 3:1-12 present the danger of a misused mouth?

4. Explain what you plan to do to prevent offense in your own life as a result of reading this chapter.

Chapter 6
Sheep Bite, but Shepherds Barbecue

Recently I was teaching on the subject of relationships and mentioned that one of the first things we learned as pastors was that "sheep bite." One of the walking wounded in the class quickly responded with, "Yes, but shepherds barbecue."

Some of the most easily offended people I know are pastors and leaders. This trait further manifests itself in their need to control and dominate their "sheep." Many wounded sheep find their way to our church because they have heard it is a safe place. This doesn't mean that we haven't hurt a few people of our own! And, yes, there have been times when I would have loved to barbecue a few sheep. However, my husband usually throws water on the coals in my barbecue pit.

Whether sheep or shepherd, we all have the ability to hurt others and become wounded. How we respond in such circumstances is more important than what the offense involves. Much of our reputation as Christians is established by how we handle offense.

Responding to offense

The initial step in responding to offense is to address our own attitudes. This isn't easy because, usually, we are wounded and not thinking clearly. However, our hearts must be right with the Lord if we want to see our actions bear fruit. The following instructions speak to our heart posture as well as to correcting actions.

> ➢ Be teachable.

"He who listens to a life-giving rebuke will be at home among the wise" (Proverbs 15:31 NIV). "A poor, yet wise lad is better than an old and foolish king who no longer knows [how] to receive instruction" (Ecclesiastes 4:13 NASB). Offense often comes when we are being confronted or corrected. Many times, I have remembered these verses after I behaved like an old and foolish king! Other times, I felt like I was right at home among the wise just because I listened and received correction. A teachable heart counters offense.

I watched Sandy sabotage one relationship after another during her four years at our church. The pattern was always the same. A friendship would blossom between Sandy and another. Eventually the friend would speak some sort of truth to Sandy concerning her lack of respect for personal boundaries. At that point, Sandy would become offended and begin to undermine the credibility of her friend to others. She would even mention a few of her own faults when talking about her friend, which made her appear sincere.

Sandy knew the teaching contained in this chapter because we had gone over it in counseling. However, practicing it was a different story. She became offended when I questioned her motives behind seemingly correct actions. Excuses and justifications became her regular response. Soon, she quit revealing all the facts concerning her damaged relationships and presented only the ones that placed her in a favorable light. Sandy's need to appear spiritual outweighed her desire for change. Finally she stopped coming to counseling and left the church. Sandy was not teachable.

> ➢ Ignore the offense.

"A fool shows his annoyance at once, but a prudent man overlooks an insult" (Proverbs 12:16 NIV). Amy Carmichael once said, "Nothing anyone can do to us can injure us unless we submit to a wrong reaction. We can't control other people, but we can control our responses."

➢   **Be quiet!**

"When words are many, sin is not absent, but he who holds his tongue is wise" (Proverbs 10:19 NIV). People will think you are wise if you just don't talk. One of the first choices we can make when offended is to just shut up! Doing this allows time for us to go before the Lord and process the offense.

➢   **Don't offend in return.**

"Do not say, 'I'll do to him as he has done to me; I'll pay that man back for what he did' " (Proverbs 24:29 NIV). Revenge and vengeance are not to be a part of kingdom relationships. Campbell McAlpine has said, "Loyalty is loyal even when others are disloyal."

➢   **Overlook the offense.**

"A man's wisdom gives him patience; it is to his glory to overlook an offense" (Proverbs 19:11 NIV). One of the most scriptural ways to receive glory is to overlook an offense. Still, not too many sermons address this method of getting glory! To overlook an offense means that we refuse to accept it. Instead, we simply look at it as it goes by. For me, this has meant to turn my head and pretend that I am watching an offense go right past me. This may seem like a silly action, but it notifies my mind and emotions that I am not going to give the offense any attention.

➢   **Forgive the offender and forget about the offense.**

"He who covers over an offense promotes love, but whoever repeats the matter separates close friends" (Proverbs 17:9 NIV). When we are offended we tend to campaign our cause to others. Of course, we feel justified in this when the offending party has clearly been in sin. Even so, the result will be division and damaged friendships. The outcome is different when we choose to cover the wrongdoing and deal with any sin in private. Choosing to forgive and then forget the transgression strengthens the bonds of love between people.

➢   Get rid of wrong attitudes and practices.

"Get rid of all bitterness, rage and anger, brawling and slander, along with every form of malice" (Ephesians 4:31 NIV). These things must not be allowed a place in our mind or emotions. They must be taken to the Cross and left there. After all, Jesus bought and paid for our hurt feelings, bitterness, rage, anger, fighting, slander, and all forms of hatred with His blood. These things are no longer ours to own! If we choose to entertain them, then we are handling something that belongs to Jesus and, technically, we should be called thieves!

➢   Actively practice the Romans 12:14-21 check list:

✓ Bless those who persecute you; bless and do not curse;

✓ Rejoice with those who rejoice; mourn with those who mourn.

✓ Live in harmony with one another.

✓ Do not be proud, but be willing to associate with people of low position. Do not be conceited.

✓ Do not repay anyone evil for evil.

✓ Be careful to do what is right in the eyes of everybody. If it is possible, as far as it depends on you, live at peace with everyone.

✓ Do not take revenge, my friends, but leave room for God's wrath, for it is written: "It is mine to avenge; I will repay," says the Lord.

✓ On the contrary: "If your enemy is hungry, feed him; if he is thirsty, give him something to drink. In doing this, you will heap burning coals on his head."

✓ Do not be overcome by evil, but overcome evil with good (NIV).

➢   Take responsibility for reconciliation.

"Therefore, if you are offering your gift at the altar and there remember that your brother has something against you, leave your gift there in front of the altar. First go and be reconciled to your brother; then come and offer your gift" (Matthew 5:23-24

NIV). If you know a brother or sister is offended with you, whether you are at fault or not, go and make peace with them. This type of spiritual responsibility can be uncomfortable, but the rewards are eternal.

The Word and warfare

There are many times when we feel we have the right to be offended. Whatever our cause is, we believe it is just. How do we process such a situation?

➢ Meditate on the Word of God.

"Though rulers sit together and slander me, your servant will meditate on your decrees" (Psalm 119:23 NIV). "May the arrogant be put to shame for wronging me without cause; but I will meditate on your precepts" (Psalm 119:78 NIV). Notice the instructions implied in these verses. We are to watch and guard our thoughts. Then we are to meditate on the Scriptures, not the offense. The way of the world would declare that we have a right to let our mind dwell on the wrongdoing, but God would have our thoughts dwell on the Scriptures.

➢ Go to prayer.

"But, O LORD Almighty, you who judge righteously and test the heart and mind, let me see your vengeance upon them, for to you I have committed my cause" (Jeremiah 11:20 NIV). Part of a biblical response to offense is to talk to God about the offense and then commit the whole situation to Him. Jeremiah sounds pretty upset in the above verse, yet he places his mind and emotions before the Lord along with his desire for vengeance.

"Cast all your anxiety on him because he cares for you" (1 Peter 5:7 NIV). It is our responsibility to transfer ownership of worries and hurts to the Lord. A friend of mine did this by driving to an isolated area outside of town. There she placed some stones in a pile and explained to the Lord how the stones represented the elders at her church who had wounded her. The stones also represented her cold, hard heart. As she prayed, she placed each stone in the ground and covered it up. She left her offenses buried in the Earth and in the hands of the Lord when she drove home. Healing came as she continued to spend time in the presence of the Lord. "He heals the brokenhearted and binds up their wounds" (Psalm 147:3 NIV).

➤   Engage in spiritual warfare.

"No weapon formed against you shall prosper, and every tongue which rises against you in judgment you shall condemn. This is the heritage of the servants of the LORD, and their righteousness is from Me, says the LORD" (Isaiah 54:17 NKJV). Remember that your fight is not against people, but against principalities and powers (see Ephesians 6:12). Spiritual warfare is required to fight spiritual enemies. In prayer you must submit yourself to God, resist demonic forces, and then expect that they will flee (see James 4:7).

At times, we have had people in the church who have spoken critically about us to others. Before we ever address the individuals involved, we confront the demonic spirits of criticism and judgment through spiritual warfare. This clears up the static in the airwaves when we connect with the individuals and process our concerns. Grace can flow, even when differences of opinion may still be present.

➤   Discuss the offense with the person who offended you.

"Debate thy cause with thy neighbor himself; and discover not a secret to another" (Proverbs 25:9 KJV). Initially, a problem should only be processed with the person who has offended you. It is not wise to involve others.

➤   If a person will not listen to your concerns, then you will have to involve a "negotiator."

"But if he will not listen, take one or two others along, so that 'every matter may be established by the testimony of two or three witnesses.' If he refuses to listen to them, tell it to the church; and if he refuses to listen even to the church, treat him as you would a pagan or a tax collector" (Matthew 18:16-17 NIV). Only after you have done all the above instructions can you involve others. This involvement is usually used for really serious sin and not the "you hurt my feelings" sort of offense. However, sometimes a negotiator works well in resolving misunderstandings between two individuals.

> ➢ Extend forgiveness, but don't feel obligated to trust.

"But if you forgive men when they sin against you, your heavenly Father will also forgive you. But if you do not forgive men their sins, your Father will not forgive your sins" (Matthew 6:14-15 NIV). To forgive someone means to release him from being under your personal judgment or debt. When forgiven, the individual no longer "owes" you anything, not even an apology.

Forgiveness is a non-negotiable issue for a Christian, but it does not require us to trust another. Forgiveness is mandatory, while trust must be earned. Do you remember the story of David and King Saul in 1 Samuel 24? Saul had been chasing David with the intent to kill him. At one point, David was able to sneak up on Saul and cut off a piece of his robe. When Saul was safely away, David confronted him about his murderous plans. King Saul repented and forgiveness was extended on both sides. As a token of his good intentions, Saul asked David to return with him to Jerusalem.

Nonetheless, David did not trust Saul and did not go back to Jerusalem with him. David continued to keep his distance from Saul by staying in his own wilderness stronghold. He obviously also kept his own counsel and remained on guard against Saul. In other words, David extended and received forgiveness from Saul and even received a prophetic confirmation from Saul. However, he refused to enter into a friendship relationship with him or even put himself under Saul's authority. Instead, he continued to respect Saul's anointing as king and refused to advance his own prophesied place as the future king. David allowed God to work all these things out in His own time. His mighty men continued to defend David, but did not try to take the kingdom. David was a man after God's own heart. He knew that trust and forgiveness are two different things.

Avoid the third-party trap

There are times when we end up becoming involved in another's offense, whether we want to or not. Below, are some instructions for when you find yourself in that position.

➢ Remember that it will be hard to be a positive negotiator.

"An offended brother is more unyielding than a fortified city, and disputes are like the barred gates of a citadel" (Proverbs 18:19 NIV). If you are the third party involved and not the one giving or receiving offense, remember that this is not your offense. Others have taken up an insult and reconciliation will be difficult. Avoid taking up the offense of another and making it your own.

➢ Show compassion to the offended.

"Who is weak without my being weak? Who is led into sin without my intense concern?" (2 Corinthians 11:29 NASB). It is all right to hurt with someone who has been offended. They need to see your concern about their wound. They also need to see your concern about the wrong way they are processing the hurt.

➢ Be loyal.

"A gossip betrays a confidence, but a trustworthy man keeps a secret" (Proverbs 11:13 NIV). Loyalty knows how to keep secrets. Try not to take sides with one person or the other. You can't move in prudence if you've taken up someone else's gripe.

➢ Use your words to bring healing.

"Reckless words pierce like a sword, but the tongue of the wise brings healing" (Proverbs 12:18 NIV). If you have to confront someone, be a channel of grace.

➢ Don't dwell on the problem.

"Anxiety in the heart of a man weighs it down, but a good word makes it glad" (Proverbs 12:25 NASB). Dwell on God's power by giving an encouraging word to the one who is wounded.

➢ Be kind.

"She opens her mouth with wisdom, and on her tongue is the law of kindness" (Proverbs 31:26 NKJV). Remember that kindness is a law that can be broken.

Remaining free of offense toward God

"And blessed is he who is not offended because of Me" (Matthew 11:6 NKJV). How difficult it is sometimes to remain free of offense even toward the Lord. Usually we become offended with God when He does not do things according to our expectations. Asking Him to forgive us for our unreal expectations is the beginning step to remaining free of offense toward Him.

The second step is to gain a realistic view of the things He allows us to go through. He is far more interested in how we respond to life situations than in freeing us from life's pressures. He has eternal plans in mind, not just the things of this lifetime. Years ago, I clipped a quote by R. Cawman out of the *Emanuel Herald*, which has helped me through many a difficult time:

> God has never shielded His own from the fury's blast. He has ever sent them out into it and asked, "Will you go out there and let the enemy do his worst and prove that Heaven has power to see you through?" The battle that tried the soul and the storm that proves the set of the sail are never that which we understand perfectly. There is no such thing as an ideal battle. Conflicts do not come in ways for which we had planned and prepared.

> When you volunteer to go with God, you volunteer to go to the depths—where understanding fails, reason quivers, the spirit shudders, and the heart cries with pain until, like Job, you say, "Though He slay me, yet will I trust Him" (Job 13:15). And out of that abyss of trial will arise a purer heart, which has its affections set more firmly on Heaven and whose treasures have been reinvested in the unfailing bank of God's love. There they are kept until this short life of testing is over and we gather on the other side of the vale to revel in the full fruition of the accumulated interest of eternal treasure that fadeth not away.

Hanging in my office is an old needlepoint stating, "No Cross, No Crown." It reminds me that every crown has a cost, and the cost of a crown for the believer is suffering. In the early part of the last century, Jessie Penn-Lewis wrote about spiritual warfare and the Christian life. I keep this quote of hers, based on Daniel 3:17-18, in my Bible:

> (My) God . . . is able to deliver from the burning fiery furnace; and He will deliver. But . . . IF NOT—I will not be offended with Him. IF NOT—He will be with me in the fire. IF NOT—Henceforth the CROWN.

Chapter application

1. Briefly explain how you plan to respond to future offenses using some of the Scriptures discussed in this chapter.

2. How would you counsel someone who appears to have a legitimate offense?

3. Why is it important to not take up the offense of another?

Chapter 7
Keeping the Peace

Jim started counseling when his sexual addiction cost him his employment. Even though Jim had done a good job of keeping his secret life concealed, it became obvious that his marriage and walk as a Christian were threatened. What concerned the counselor was that Jim thought his sexual addiction was something he could control. Therefore, he didn't understand how much it contaminated his marriage and his relationship with God. Slowly Jim began the process of inner healing and restoration.

The journey involved learning a whole new way of kingdom thinking and conduct. Accountability was imperative. The support of friends and leadership kept Jim encouraged and moving toward full recovery. Thankfully, he embraced that recovery process, and today, Jim is part of a group of men helping others heal from sexual addictions. He also leads a ministry team at his church.

This story might have ended differently if Jim had been involved in a church that rejected those contaminated with sin or ignored the seriousness of the problem. While most churches would have handled the situation in a manner similar to the way Jim's did, unfortunately, we have known fellowships where the leadership did not deal properly with those caught in sin. In some cases, it was those in leadership positions who remained in sin and refused to become accountable.

The Bible is a book about reconciliation and restoration between man and God and between man and others. It is filled with instructions and has plenty of examples of what happens to those who follow the instructions and those who don't. For a believer, reconciliation and restoration are ongoing experiences that need to be clearly understood if we are to be ministers of both. As it was the foremost ministry of Jesus, so should it be ours. We must be willing to do whatever it takes to see reconciliation and restoration happen among those with whom we associate.

> As a prisoner for the Lord, then, I urge you to live a life worthy of the calling you have received. Be completely humble and gentle; be patient, bearing with one another in love. Make every effort to keep the unity of the Spirit through the bond of peace (Ephesians 4:1-3 NIV).

The ministry of reconciliation and restoration

To *reconcile* means that positive change happens between those who stand in opposition to each other. No longer do they oppose each other, but they stand in favor with one another. The Bible speaks of this when it talks of God and man being reconciled through the work of Jesus Christ:

> For if, when we were God's enemies, we were reconciled to him through the death of his Son, how much more, having been reconciled, shall we be saved through his life (Romans 5:10 NIV).

> And although you were formerly alienated and hostile in mind, [engaged] in evil deeds, yet He has now reconciled you in His fleshly body through death, in order to present you before Him holy and blameless and beyond reproach (Colossians 1:21-22 NASB).

Because we now have experienced reconciliation ourselves, God calls us in 2 Corinthians 5:18-19 to continue this ministry in our relationships with others. "Now all [these] things are from God, who reconciled us to Himself through Christ, and gave us the ministry of reconciliation, namely, that God was in Christ reconciling the world to Himself, not counting their trespasses against them, and He has committed to us the word of reconciliation" (NASB).

We are to be people who refuse to allow enmity to exist between others and ourselves. A Christian should be able to enter a situation and help those who stand in opposition to God, or to each other, so they can become changed and reconciled.

After reconciliation has occurred, restoration is needed. *Restoration* carries the idea of repairing or renewing a relationship from what has been damaged to the condition originally intended by God. Reconciliation removes enmity and brings favor, but restoration goes beyond that change and deals with the ruin that has happened in the relationship. It endeavors to rebuild into God's design that which has been destroyed.

The Greek word for restore is *katartizo*. It was a medical term used for mending a broken bone. It also was a military term for outfitting a fleet of ships, or equipping an army. In a personal manner, restore meant to bring harmony in a family. And finally, restore was a fishing term used by fishermen for sewing nets together that had been torn. All of these are word descriptions for the type of actions that are needed to help a person rebuild their relationship with God and with other people.

Scripture gives us very practical instruction in both reconciliation and restoration. In addressing reconciliation, the Scripture speaks of confrontation of sin, confession of sin to one another, and extending forgiveness in our relationships. For restoration, we are given specific things that can be done to see wholeness brought to our relationships. Instructions are given on how to deny the sin nature and walk in the power of the Holy Spirit. Choices are identified that can help us change our unhealthy thinking and acting. Accountability is another important part of restoration as we learn to allow others to speak into our lives.

Isaiah 61:1-4 speaks of this ministry of reconciliation and restoration. The first and second verses describe the work of *reconciliation*, where enmity is removed and favor established. "The Spirit of the Lord GOD is upon me, because the LORD has anointed me to bring good news to the afflicted; He has sent me to bind up the brokenhearted, to proclaim liberty to captives, and freedom to prisoners; To proclaim the favorable year of the LORD, and the day of vengeance of our God; to comfort all who mourn" (NASB).

Verses three and four describe the ministry of *restoration* in the lives of those who have been reconciled. "To grant those who mourn [in] Zion, giving them a garland instead of ashes, the oil of gladness instead of mourning, the mantle of praise instead of a spirit of fainting. So they will be called oaks of righteousness, the planting of the LORD, that He may be glorified. Then they will rebuild the ancient ruins, they will raise up the former devastations, and they will repair the ruined cities, the desolations of many generations" (NASB).

Confession and repentance of sin

Some time ago, a pastor from our area moved to a different state. I was relieved to see him go. He had earned a reputation for wounding those under his care and many of these people ended up in other churches throughout our community. Several pastors, including my husband, had tried to negotiate for reconciliation between these people and the pastor. Unfortunately, his response was rude and disrespectful.

In a few instances, this man offered a general apology to those he had hurt. Each time, he failed to acknowledge that he had done anything wrong. No sin was identified. His response was, "I'm sorry if we had a misunderstanding." Reconciliation was not a concept with which this pastor was familiar.

In order for a person to repent, sin must first be confessed by the person who carried out the sin. *Confession* means to acknowledge that a specific sin was committed so that repentance can then take place. *Repentance* is the action of asking God and others for forgiveness for that particular sin. For example, a wife might say to her husband, "I was wrong to have lost my temper and shouted at you in front of the children. Will you please forgive me?"

Ignoring, excusing, or justifying sin hinders reconciliation. It is not confession or repentance for someone to say, "I'm sorry *if* I have wronged you." This response does not identify the sin, nor is the person taking ownership of the sin. Responsibility is being shifted back to the other party. Ownership of sin is important because, without ownership, we do not have the right to transfer that sin over to Jesus—the One who bought and paid for the sin with His blood. Nor can we receive forgiveness for something that we are implying may not really be ours. Once we confess sin before Jesus, it becomes His, and forgiveness is given in exchange for that sin.

> If we claim to be without sin, we deceive ourselves and the truth is not in us. If we confess our sins, he is faithful and just and will forgive us our sins and purify us from all unrighteousness. If we claim we have not sinned, we make him out to be a liar and his word has no place in our lives (1 John 1:8-10 NIV).

Repentance of sin is an important part of reconciliation because healing is tied closely to confession. James 5:16 explains it this way: "Therefore confess your sins to each other and pray for each other so that you may be healed. The prayer of a righteous man is powerful and effective" (NIV).

Seldom do we find that only one person is at fault in a relationship where reconciliation needs to take place. Usually there is something that each party needs to own, repent of, and seek forgiveness for. Even when we know that one party is blameless, there always needs to be an atmosphere of grace surrounding the reconciliation process.

Extending forgiveness

> Then Peter came to Him and said, "Lord, how often shall my brother sin against me, and I forgive him? Up to seven times?" Jesus said to him, "I do not say to you, up to seven times, but up to seventy times seven" (Matthew 18:21-22 NKJ).

Extending forgiveness is never an option in the kingdom of God, regardless of how many times we have to forgive someone. It doesn't matter if the person has confessed or repented of their sin against us; God expects us to forgive! In fact, we will be judged in Heaven based on how we have extended forgiveness here on Earth. Forgiveness is the foundation on which every problem is processed within the kingdom.

> For if you forgive men when they sin against you, your heavenly Father will also forgive you. But if you do not forgive men their sins, your Father will not forgive your sins (Matthew 6:14-15 NIV).

> Bearing with one another, and forgiving one another, if anyone has a complaint against another; even as Christ forgave you, so you also must do (Colossians 3:13 NKJV).

The Greek and Hebrew words for *forgive* include the meaning of "sending away." Jesus sent away our sins to the Cross when He forgave us. He didn't just ignore or overlook our sins. He actively did something about them. We are to do the same thing when we forgive another. In our heart and mind, we are to send away their sin against us. We send it to the Cross and leave it there. That sin now belongs to Jesus, who bought and paid for it. It is no longer any of our business!

Forgiveness is a choice and not a feeling. Extending forgiveness does not mean that we will forget the transgression. Philippians 3:13 directs us to forget the things that lie behind and focus on the things before us. However, the word translated *forget* in this passage is better translated, *neglecting*. When we forgive someone, we are to stop thinking about the offense, or neglect it. As we continue to place our focus elsewhere, the offense will fade in our memory.

Pam had forgiven Tim for his years of involvement with pornography and their marriage was in a healthy process of restoration. Sexual sin no longer held Tim captive as he continued to attend his purity group for accountability. They were receiving counseling to help bring trust and communication back into their marriage. Still, Pam and Tim slept in different rooms. Haunting memories and rejection kept

75

her from fulfilling the most intimate relationship of marriage. However, Pam knew it was time to trust again. She made a choice to obey 1 Corinthians 7:3-4: "The husband should fulfill his marital duty to his wife, and likewise the wife to her husband. The wife's body does not belong to her alone but also to her husband. In the same way, the husband's body does not belong to him alone but also to his wife" (NIV).

Pam's obedience broke the stalemate in their marriage. It became easier for her to stop thinking about the past. Old memories began to be replaced with positive moments that slowly filled her mental scrapbook. Today their marriage is a testimony to reconciliation and restoration.

Putting a time limit on anger

At times, anger can be a positive force to help us face a situation needing to be addressed. Left unattended, however, anger can be detrimental to reconciliation and restoration. "Be angry, and [yet] do not sin; do not let the sun go down on your anger, and do not give the devil an opportunity" (Ephesians 4:26-27 NASB).

Anger, whether righteous or sinful, is given a time limit in the life of a kingdom person. We are not to allow anger to last past sundown! If we do, we give the devil an opportunity to grab hold of our thoughts and emotions, thereby gaining a foothold in our lives.

Anger can be internalized and pent up. Such anger is very unwise and dangerous to us, personally, and eventually damages our relationships. Anger expressed outwardly in harmful ways can be destructive to ourselves and to those around us, as it shows a lack of the fruit of the Spirit of self-control. That is why, in the culture of the kingdom, anger is never allowed much time to ferment.

Before sundown, we are to do whichever of the following is necessary for peace and proper handling of a situation: repent, forgive, and/or plan a course of action that will fulfill scriptural instruction for reconciliation.

It is also important to take our thoughts captive and refuse to allow them to dwell on the situation in an unwholesome way. We are to focus our thoughts on kingdom ways of thinking according to Philippians 4:8:

> Finally, brethren, whatever is true, whatever is honorable, whatever is right, whatever is pure, whatever is lovely, whatever is of good repute, if there is any excellence and if anything worthy of praise, let your mind dwell on these things (NASB).

The key is to always look at a situation that has caused anger with the attitude, "How can I best represent Jesus in this situation?" Remember, at any given point in time and with any person, believer or unbeliever, you are a representative of the kingdom of God and kingdom principles. Your life is a living testimony of what the King and kingdom are all about!

Many find it helpful to plan a course of action for the next time they run into a problem with anger. For example, using the "if / then" model, I might decide that: "*If* my husband comes home moody again, *then* I will not become angry at him for making me feel like I have to walk on eggshells around him. I will recognize that it is his problem and not mine. I will be kind and considerate and, at an appropriate time, ask him if anything is bothering him."

Practicing the "put off and put on" principle

Restoration always involves change. Old ways of thinking and relating to others must change into kingdom ways. This process involves identifying what the old ways of thinking and acting might be. As they are identified, they can be repented of and new ways learned and practiced. In such a manner, we are deciding to "put off" the ways of the sin nature and "put on" the ways of God. We do this through casting down arguments, or wrong processes of reasoning, and renewing the mind. We then adjust our actions accordingly.

> Casting down arguments and every high thing that exalts itself against the knowledge of God, bringing

every thought into captivity to the obedience of Christ (2 Corinthians 10:5 NKJV).

And do not be conformed to this world, but be transformed by the renewing of your mind, that you may prove what the will of God is, that which is good and acceptable and perfect (Romans 12:2 NASB).

Notice how Paul explains the put off and put on principle and gives practical examples in Ephesians 4:22-32:

You were taught, with regard to your former way of life, to put off your old self, which is being corrupted by its deceitful desires; to be made new in the attitude of your minds; and to put on the new self, created to be like God in true righteousness and holiness.

Therefore each of you must put off falsehood and speak truthfully to his neighbor, for we are all members of one body. "In your anger do not sin": Do not let the sun go down while you are still angry, and do not give the devil a foothold. He who has been stealing must steal no longer, but must work, doing something useful with his own hands, that he may have something to share with those in need. Do not let any unwholesome talk come out of your mouths, but only what is helpful for building others up according to their needs, that it may benefit those who listen. And do not grieve the Holy Spirit of God, with whom you were sealed for the day of redemption.

Get rid of all bitterness, rage and anger, brawling and slander, along with every form of malice. Be kind and compassionate to one another, forgiving each other, just as in Christ God forgave you (NIV).

The put off and put on principle is one we will practice many times as we see things in Scripture that require us to change. It is also something we must instruct others in as they move from reconciliation into restoration. Kingdom attitudes and actions do not happen automatically, even when reconciliation has been successful. Restoration often requires concentrated attention and accountability in forming new ways of thinking and acting.

There is no perfect church or family. We will always have to help each other clean up our sin messes, but that is part of living together and seeing the kingdom of God advance. Proverb 14:4 states it this way: "Where no oxen are, the manger is clean, but much increase [comes] by the strength of the ox" (NASB). My husband has often said that ministry would be great if it weren't for the people! In the next chapter, we will look at different ways to handle the people problems that invariably occur when more than one of us gather together in His name.

Chapter application

1. Describe one situation where you have practiced the ministry of reconciliation. What did you do after reconciliation to see restoration happen in the lives of those reconciled?

2. Describe an area in your life where you have an anger problem. Plan a course of action for the next time you run into this problem using the if / then model.

3. Make a list of habits that you need to put off. Next to each one, write a godly habit that you need to put on.

Chapter 8
What Do I Do When . . . ?

This was the second time Alice had come to the Sunday night service drunk. One of the ushers and his wife took her home and helped her get settled for the night. The next day, they reconnected Alice with the local Alcoholic Anonymous group. She had been attending the group for three years, but had quit during the last six months.

Initially, Alice felt foolish and embarrassed and wouldn't return the phone calls of her church friends. She grew angry with the usher and his wife who had helped her, and she was sure they were gossiping about her at church. This couple continued to love Alice, and often invited her to Sunday services. Eventually, she began attending church again and found a warm welcome among old friends. Looking back at this time in her life, Alice is thankful her friends did not give up on her when she was being so difficult. The usher and his wife are now among her closest companions.

All of us can look back at relationships we have mishandled. We have all made mistakes. This is normal. It is acceptable to fail, as long as we evaluate our failures and learn from them. The process of reconciliation and restoration allows for positive growth in the midst of difficult relationships. In addition, the Scriptures give us various directions for approaching circumstances where people are the problem. Not every situation is handled the same way.

What do I do when someone I know is caught in sin?

"Brothers, if someone is caught in a sin, you who are spiritual should restore him gently. But watch yourself, or you also may be tempted" (Galatians 6:1 NIV). This verse is describing a person who has repeated a mistake enough times for it to become a personal fault or identifying mark in their life. The story of Alice is one of a person caught in sin. Her life was unproductive and she was gaining the reputation of a drunk. She had made a deliberate choice that was dictating her life. Other times a sin might not be so overt. Individuals may subtly step aside from their Christian journey. Either way, sin has overtaken them and they become trapped, unable to get free.

The one commanded to help is the person who is spiritual. A spiritual person is anyone who is responsive to and controlled by the Holy Spirit. Any believer can meet these qualifications. This might be anyone, that is, if their known sins are confessed and they are walking in dependence before the Lord. It isn't just the pastor and elders called to assist the trapped brother or sister! For Alice, the usher and his wife were the ones God used to help her find freedom.

The way the trapped person is to be approached is with gentleness. Each of us has areas where we also could become trapped at any time if we are not watchful, so our attitude must be one of humbleness and meekness. Alice's friends continued to approach her with gentleness, even when she was rejecting them. Their patience won her heart.

What do I do when there exists unresolved issues between a fellow believer and myself?

Matthew 5:23-24 gives us clear instructions on how to address such a situation. "Therefore, if you are offering your gift at the altar and there remember that your brother has something against you, leave your gift there in front of the altar. First go and be reconciled to your brother; then come and offer your gift" (NIV).

Note that the unresolved issue isn't necessarily stated as a sin committed by you. All you know is that your brother or sister has an offense against you. The issue is not whose fault it is— the issue is that it is there at all! The urgency for reconciliation is emphasized by the fact that you are not to continue in worship until reconciliation has happened. Reconciliation is so important to God that He considers it more important than worship! Jay Adams states, "Unreconciled relationships, therefore, constitute emergency priorities that may not be handled casually or at one's leisure."

The responsibility to go and seek reconciliation is yours alone— no excuses or justifications. In Scripture, it is always your obligation to make the first move! And yes, it is also your brother's responsibility. However, you won't have to answer to God for your brother's obedience or disobedience, only your own!

In our church we consider this principle so important we have instituted the practice of *heart check*. No one is allowed to minister as part of the worship team, intercession team, or other ministry teams without having first dealt with any unresolved issues between themselves and others, on or off the team. This heart check-up is done whenever the teams meet for meetings or ministry. Team members are expected to deal with their people problems before they are allowed to minister to God or others. If God considers relationships such a priority, so do we.

What do I do when someone sins against me, yet refuses to acknowledge it?

What does reconciliation and restoration look like in such a situation? Matthew 18:15-17 addresses this question through a process of four steps. Because this passage uses the term *brother*, it is a reconciliation process that is used in Christian relationships. However, the first two steps would apply to any relationship, regardless if the individuals are believers.

Step One: "If your brother sins against you, go and show him his fault, just between the two of you. If he listens to you, you have won your brother over" (Matthew 18:15 NIV).

Note that this action is a private one and could involve more than one meeting. Usually, step one is all that is needed in ministering reconciliation. Sometimes, communication has broken down to the point of needing a negotiator to intervene in the process. Only at that point, should we move on to the second part of the Matthew 18 instructions.

Step Two: "But if he will not listen, take one or two others along, so that 'every matter may be established by the testimony of two or three witnesses' " (Matthew 18:16 NIV).

In a reconciliation process, the negotiators should do all that is possible to straighten out the situation. They are there to clarify matters and bring resolve between the two individuals. Assumptions are separated from facts, and repentance and forgiveness are sought. Negotiators also stand as witnesses to whatever is said or happens. If their involvement fails to bring reconciliation, only then do the negotiators take the matter to the church leadership.

Step Three: "If he refuses to listen to them, tell it to the church" (Matthew 18:17 NIV).

Church discipline now becomes the focus instead of reconciliation, yet even such discipline is aimed at reconciliation. The purpose of all discipline is to see individuals brought back into right relationship with God and with people (see 1 Timothy 1:20; 2 Thessalonians 3:14, 15; 1 Corinthians 5:5). If step three doesn't bring reconciliation, then step four is the final attempt at reconciliation.

Step Four: "And if he refuses to listen even to the church, treat him as you would a pagan or a tax collector" (Matthew 18:17 NIV).

If repentance happens at any point in the working of these four steps, the process is terminated. The corporate church, meaning the eldership and the whole fellowship, doesn't become involved until possibly step two, and definitely in steps three

83

and four. Step three of "tell it to the church" is always processed through the leadership of the church, who then communicates it to the congregation. Counseling and accountability will be necessary in fulfilling the last two steps of Matthew 18, especially when someone has committed sexual immorality, murder, financial misconduct, slander, or any other grievous sin.

What do I do if a person is causing division in my family, workplace, church, or other arena?

If anyone teaches otherwise and does not consent to wholesome words, even the words of our Lord Jesus Christ, and to the doctrine which accords with godliness, he is proud, knowing nothing, but is obsessed with disputes and arguments over words, from which come envy, strife, reviling, evil suspicions, useless wranglings of men of corrupt minds and destitute of the truth, who suppose that godliness is a means of gain. From such withdraw yourself (1 Timothy 6:3-5 NKJV).

But avoid foolish controversies and genealogies and arguments and quarrels about the law, because these are unprofitable and useless. Warn a divisive person once, and then warn him a second time. After that, have nothing to do with him (Titus 3:9-10 NIV).

Some years ago, we had a gentleman in our fellowship that began to undermine the leadership. His conversations put doubt in people's minds concerning the ability of the pastors and elders to lead. Rather than bring his concerns to those he was criticizing, he explained that he was a prophet and had more insight than the leaders. His warm and seemingly loving personality combined with his critical comments brought confusion to the congregation and we began to hear about it.

When two of our elders approached him with a warning, he humbly submitted to their counsel. However, a few months later, we discovered he was still talking to folks about his personal belief that the leadership was out of God's will. The elders warned him again and he appeared to be receptive to their advice. The third time we learned he was attempting to cause division he was asked to leave.

A person who is causing factions and division should be warned twice. If you find no positive response, withdraw yourself from fellowship with them. If you are in a position of authority, ask them to withdraw themselves from the fellowship or ministry you oversee. If the person is a family member, you may have to leave the room or ask them to leave the room. Children need to be separated and sent to a different room when they cause divisions among siblings. Teens who are over 18 years old and are consistently causing division in the home should be asked to relocate. A spouse may need to consent to marriage counseling. A co-worker may find that you will relate to him only on a professional basis and refuse to give him the attention of friendship.

Simple personal offenses, such as personality clashes and the causing of hurt feelings, can be processed according to Proverbs 19:11 and 12:16 where we are told to overlook, or ignore, an offense. "A man's wisdom gives him patience; it is to his glory to overlook an offense" (Proverbs 19:11 NIV). "A fool shows his annoyance at once, but a prudent man overlooks an insult" (Proverbs 12:16 NIV).

What if there is a personality clash or difference of opinion between another and myself?

In the New Testament, Paul and John Mark fit this description. Something happened in their relationship or in their definition of Paul's mission that caused a breach. We know it wasn't serious sin, such as immorality or slander on John Mark's side, or Paul would have applied Matthew 18 to the problem with John Mark. Instead, Paul simply asked John Mark to not be a part of his ministry.

Barnabas disagreed with Paul concerning John Mark and also quit traveling with Paul's ministry because of his views. One has the feeling from Scripture that this was an "agree to disagree" parting. Later, Paul changed his mind about John Mark and requested his participation in Paul's Gentile ministry.

Personality clashes are not sin—how they are expressed can be. In an agree to disagree parting, it is important that grace and respect be the flow of the disagreement. If things have been processed improperly, then repentance and forgiveness are necessary. However, one doesn't have to repent or forgive for their personal opinion. Unity doesn't mean that we have to agree about everything!

What if none of this works?

Only after we have seriously tried to seek reconciliation according to the Scriptures may we acknowledge an irreconcilable situation. Romans 12:18 states, "If it is possible, as far as it depends on you, live at peace with everyone" (NIV). There will be times when we cannot live at peace with someone even after we have followed all of God's instructions. At such a point, we must acknowledge that we are still trusting God to bring a place of reconciliation. As much as possible, we need to continue to seek peace in the situation and not aggravate it further.

Chapter application

1. Think of someone you know who is trapped in some kind of sin. Then personalize Galatians 6:1 in your own words.

2. Are there any relationships in your life right now where you know that the other person has an offense against you or has been hurt by you? Are there unresolved issues between you and another? Write out a plan of action that you can fulfill this week to see reconciliation happen. Remember: this is more important to God than worship!

Chapter 9
How To Get Along With a Pharisee

"Home schooling is not the Gospel! Sending your children to public school does not determine where they will spend eternity!"

How often I have wanted to say these words to some on the front lines of teaching their children at home. They usually are unaware of the unspoken message behind their personal campaign for home education.

We have home schooled our children for many years. Others of our friends have their children in public school. How a person educates his children should be a private, family matter. Unfortunately, we have run into believers who feel that if a child is not home schooled, than the parents are out of the will of God. Their attitude communicates that those who send their children to public school are second-class Christians.

We have seen the same attitude toward women who choose to work outside the home. Apparently, to some, stay-at-home moms are more spiritual than those who seek a career. And Heaven help the church that baptizes infants, speaks in tongues, or doesn't recognize the ministry of a prophet! Our legalistic attitudes divide our families and our church communities.

Modern day Pharisees

One of the places where grace should be most evident is in our relationships with other believers. It is a logical assumption to believe that we will find grace flowing freely between

Christians. Unfortunately, that is not the situation. In many churches and in many relationships, we instead find the ministry of judgment operating. This problem is usually tied to extra-biblical beliefs and issues.

Extra-biblical issues are principles, ideals, rules and standards that are not directly commanded of us in the Scriptures. These are men's efforts, in every generation, to make God's Word applicable to our lives. For instance, how to take communion is never prescribed in the New Testament. Men, therefore, have stepped in and made rules. Jesus gave the command: "Do this in remembrance of Me." Men made the extra-biblical rule: Do it once a week or the first of each month.

Baptism is another obvious example. Christ says, "Baptize them . . ." Men deal in the extra-biblical when they say "by immersion" or "by sprinkling." Other extra-biblical issues might be public education versus home schooling, courtship versus dating, or what is appropriate music, food, or dress for the Christian.

There is nothing wrong with extra-biblical positions until what is extra-biblical contradicts or is equated with Scripture and called the absolute will of God. It is at this point that extra-biblical ideas become toxic. Paul wrestled with the Galatians over this issue. His conclusion is that the extra-biblical demands that we place upon others or ourselves concerning areas not commanded in Scripture always bring about divisions, biting, and devouring (see Galatians 5:11-15). God grieves over the disputes, dissensions, and factions, which are the result of taking rigid stands on doctrines and practices that are marginal in importance to our faith.

Jesus kept running into the extra-biblical standards of those in the party of Jews called the Pharisees. The word *Pharisee* means "separatist." A Pharisee sought to separate himself from anything that would contaminate or cause him to compromise with evil.

A familiar example is how the Sabbath commandment, "Remember the Sabbath day and keep it holy," was altered. In Jesus' day, 39 additional laws—or extra-biblical standards based upon this fourth commandment—were added by these separatists and regarded as the equivalent of the command itself. If one was going to truly keep the Sabbath holy, then obedience meant one couldn't ride a beast or light a fire, sexual intimacy with your spouse was canceled, and no plucking of grain as Jesus did on the Sabbath day was performed (see Luke 6:1-2).

Paul addressed this problem in Romans, chapter 14:

> Accept him whose faith is weak, without passing judgment on disputable matters. One man's faith allows him to eat everything, but another man, whose faith is weak, eats only vegetables. The man who eats everything must not look down on him who does not, and the man who does not eat everything must not condemn the man who does, for God has accepted him. Who are you to judge someone else's servant? To his own master he stands or falls. And he will stand, for the Lord is able to make him stand.

> One man considers one day more sacred than another; another man considers every day alike. Each one should be fully convinced in his own mind. He who regards one day as special, does so to the Lord. He who eats meat, eats to the Lord, for he gives thanks to God; and he who abstains, does so to the Lord and gives thanks to God.

> For none of us lives to himself alone and none of us dies to himself alone. If we live, we live to the Lord; and if we die, we die to the Lord. So, whether we live or die, we belong to the Lord. For this very reason, Christ died and returned to life so that he might be the Lord of both the dead and the living.

> You, then, why do you judge your brother? Or why do you look down on your brother? For we will all stand before God's judgment seat. It is written: " 'As surely as I live,' says the Lord, 'every knee will bow before me; every tongue will confess to God.' " So then, each of us will give an account of himself to God. Therefore

let us stop passing judgment on one another. Instead, make up your mind not to put any stumbling block or obstacle in your brother's way.

As one who is in the Lord Jesus, I am fully convinced that no food is unclean in itself. But if anyone regards something as unclean, then for him it is unclean. If your brother is distressed because of what you eat, you are no longer acting in love. Do not by your eating destroy your brother for whom Christ died. Do not allow what you consider good to be spoken of as evil. For the kingdom of God is not a matter of eating and drinking, but of righteousness, peace and joy in the Holy Spirit, because anyone who serves Christ in this way is pleasing to God and approved by men.

Let us therefore make every effort to do what leads to peace and to mutual edification. Do not destroy the work of God for the sake of food. All food is clean, but it is wrong for a man to eat anything that causes someone else to stumble. It is better not to eat meat or drink wine or to do anything else that will cause your brother to fall.

So whatever you believe about these things keep between yourself and God. Blessed is the man who does not condemn himself by what he approves. But the man who has doubts is condemned if he eats, because his eating is not from faith; and everything that does not come from faith is sin (NIV).

In our fellowship, we have friends who do not celebrate Christmas, as they believe it is a pagan holiday. Our family happens to enjoy the season and we decorate our house to the max. Rather than let this be an issue that divides us, we have found that respecting each other's values concerning the holiday season draws us closer. They usually skip the Christmas service at church and instead we celebrate our friendship by going out to lunch together. We have agreed to disagree and to honor one another in the process.

Ephesians 4:4-6 lists the following seven essential things that all believers share in common: one body, one Spirit, one hope, one Lord, one faith, one baptism, and one God and Father. To bring division between brothers and sisters over issues not on this list is to sin. That is why we are exhorted to, "preserve the unity of the Spirit in the bond of peace." How we do this is through walking with one another in humility, gentleness, patience, and forbearance. Grace is extended toward others when we treat them according to Ephesians 4:1-6:

> I, therefore, the prisoner of the Lord, entreat you to walk in a manner worthy of the calling with which you have been called, with all humility and gentleness, with patience, showing forbearance to one another in love, being diligent to preserve the unity of the Spirit in the bond of peace. [There is] one body and one Spirit, just as also you were called in one hope of your calling; one Lord, one faith, one baptism, one God and Father of all who is over all and through all and in all (NASB).

Throughout his book, *The Practice of Godliness*, Jerry Bridges defines humility, gentleness, patience, and forbearance: *Humility* is the ability to look beyond our position and self, recognizing the value and worth of others. *Gentleness* is the ability to deal with others in mildness, having a sensitive regard for others, careful never to be unfeeling toward their rights, but showing respect for their personal dignity. *Patience* is the ability to suffer a long time under the mistreatment of others without growing resentful or bitter. *Forbearance* is the gracious tolerance of others' faults, failures, and the disappointments they have caused us.[ii]

In his chapter on gentleness, Jerry comments, "Paul's admonition in Philippians 4:5 provides the proper motivation for a considerate attitude. 'Let your gentleness (or considerateness) be evident to all. The Lord is near.' We might rephrase it, 'The Lord is standing at my shoulder, waiting to see how I will handle the various relationships I have with people today. Will I be rigid and exacting in my demands of them? Or will I be gentle and considerate, seeking to understand the pressures and insecurities they face and making allowances accordingly?' We are to show consideration to all—the store clerk, the bus driver, family members, non-Christians as well as Christians."[iii]

Paula often comes down to the church on Saturday afternoons to spend a few hours playing the piano in worship. She believes that Saturday is the Sabbath and this is her way of keeping it holy. Mike, her husband, believes that Sunday is the New Testament Sabbath and he and the kids, along with Paula, attend Sunday service. Paula's additional involvement at church on Sundays is one of the ways she honors her husband and others who believe differently from her concerning the Sabbath.

Our youth pastor has spiky hair, earrings, and likes rock music—quite the fashion for a young man in 2003. To some believers, this might seem blasphemous. We think it is great, especially when so many young people see Jesus in him and become Christians because of his influence. The culture of the kingdom of God radiates from within Colby's life and he feels free to dress according to the world's culture to win the lost. The kids know the difference. They initially connect with his choice of style, but then are hooked into a relationship with Jesus through Colby's humility, gentleness, and patience.

A modern day Pharisee is called a legalist. They tend to view grace as a license and allowance for sin. That, however, is not the biblical picture of grace in relationships. For one who has truly tasted grace, license will be regarded as repugnant and an insult to true grace.

In Psalm 119:29, David asks the Lord to "grant me thy law graciously." If God did not give us His Word graciously, it would kill us. God can say some very hard things to us when we have received His grace. Legalism is simply an opinion of God's will with grace removed. We can appear legalistic if grace does not precede, cover, and follow our dealings and communication with others.

A legalist is someone who has placed himself in the judge's chair but neglected to wear the title of grace. He has a hard time allowing others the freedom to fail. A judge that presides in condemnation cannot accomplish reconciliation for another. He just likes to give the verdict: guilty and condemned.

To judge or not to judge

There are times when God calls us to evaluate or judge others. Parents have this responsibility over their children, as does an employer over an employee. However, the requirement that accompanies that authority is that we evaluate under the kingdom title of Judge Grace. A judge who presides in grace will maintain justice and accomplish reconciliation and restoration.

If we pass judgment on others where we have no authority, then we become a busybody, which is forbidden in 1 Peter 4:15. Derek Prince states that, "A busybody is someone who has made himself an overseer over matters which have not been given him to oversee."

Evaluations that criticize, condemn, and have no motive of restoration communicate a rejection of another. If we move in this type of judgment, we will reap it in our own lives. Notice how Jesus addresses the issue of improper judgment with clarity and firmness, yet adds instructions about proper judgment in Matthew 7:1-6.

> Do not judge, or you too will be judged. For in the same way you judge others, you will be judged, and with the measure you use, it will be measured to you. Why do you look at the speck of sawdust in your brother's eye and pay no attention to the plank in your own eye? How can you say to your brother, "Let me take the speck out of your eye," when all the time there is a plank in your own eye? You hypocrite, first take the plank out of your own eye, and then you will see clearly to remove the speck from your brother's eye. Do not give dogs what is sacred; do not throw your pearls to pigs. If you do, they may trample them under their feet, and then turn and tear you to pieces (NIV).

Jesus isn't saying we shouldn't judge others, just that we should not do it outside of grace, and first dealing with our own issues.

Righteous judgment is a type of evaluation. Note how Jesus goes on to give instructions about where we deposit our pearls after His instructions about not judging. His instructions include making an evaluation on what is sacred and what is not. Then He tells us not to give special things, or pearls, to that which we have judged as unholy—the pigs. Notice also that He doesn't instruct us to call the pigs, "pigs." Just make the evaluation not to place your pearls in their vicinity and move on. This is grace in action.

Righteous judgment always brings reconciliation and freedom. Unrighteous judgment brings bondage. When unrighteous judgment is present in a relationship, a person will feel bound and unable to freely be himself. When we move in judgment against another, we create a wall between us and the other person. When we move in grace and forgiveness, the wall is removed and the relationship is free to flourish. The decision is ours. It is in the midst of a discussion on relationships that Matthew 18:18 talks about binding and loosing. "I tell you the truth, whatever you bind on earth will be bound in heaven, and whatever you loose on earth will be loosed in heaven" (NIV).

You may have sensed this yourself. How often have you been with a parent or relative and felt yourself regress into childhood dictates of interacting? If you have been under a parent's judgment of worthlessness, you will feel worthless whenever you spend time with them. Your responses and actions will communicate your bondage. A friend who has judged you as silly and of little importance will find that you always seem to be so around her. In each case, judgment has bound the relationship.

It is only as we are loosed from another's personal judgment that we are free to be ourselves around them. In the same way, as we loose others from our personal opinions through forgiveness, we bring freedom to our relationship with them. We either are in the business of freeing people or bringing bondage to people. How do people perceive you? What do you bring to your relationships?

One area that this can be especially damaging in is giving a word of the Lord to another. If we believe that we have the mind of the Lord for someone and it doesn't ring true to that person, then we must never put it forth with the attitude of, "Thus saith the Lord; I've heard from God, and I'm right, and you are wrong." Such a judgmental opinion is very destructive among believers.

A word of knowledge or wisdom, as well as prophecy or godly counsel, should always be presented in grace. If the information doesn't sound like Jesus to the recipient, ask him to shelve the word and reconsider it later. Perhaps you didn't hear the Lord correctly. Perhaps they aren't at a place of seeing it yet. Either way, the dignity of the individual needs to be valued, as it is his choice to receive the word or reject it, which is one of the greatest gifts of God to man—free will.

We must not walk away from such an encounter with a superior attitude as "one who sees" opposing "one who is blind." Otherwise, the godly counsel will bring bondage. We never have the Lord's permission to make ourselves His messenger when we lack grace and move in assumption or judgment in His name, nor should we believe that we always hear the Lord correctly. You don't—so don't assume you do. That is called pride, which is another avenue for bringing bondage.

It is ultimately our choice concerning how we receive another's opinion. We can choose to be offended or we can choose to overlook a judgmental attitude. If we choose to respond in grace to whatever comes our way, we will find ourselves walking in freedom even if others are not. Eleanor Roosevelt wisely stated, "No one can make you feel inferior without your consent."

Chapter application

1. How would you counsel a Christian who has allowed their personal convictions to separate them from other believers who have different opinions?

2. According to Matthew 7:1-6, what criteria did Jesus give for the privilege of counseling another concerning their blindness?

Chapter 10
Attila the Hun and Doris Doormat

It took about a month of counseling before Amber could trust me enough to tell me her story. Her walls were up and her emotional gates closed to anyone who represented authority. Amber had been involved in a church with an engaging pastor and committed people. At first, Amber was drawn to the church because it seemed to be on the cutting edge of what God was doing. In fact, the pastor reminded her of her father who had also been a strong leader. Amber felt at home with the people, the pastor, and the exciting things God seemed to be doing in the fellowship.

However, as time passed, Amber began to realize that something was wrong. Pastoral decisions were never to be questioned, as one was taught not to "touch God's anointed." People could not attend conferences or other churches without pastoral approval. Whenever Amber missed a Sunday service, a phone call was received from the pastor asking where she had been. Amber submitted to this because it felt somewhat normal. Her father had ruled his family with the same type of authority. Growing up, Amber had learned that being submissive meant to obey without thinking for herself and to never voice an opinion different from her father's.

When Amber decided to leave the church, she was labeled by the leadership as rebellious, and she was put on the church blacklist. Others still in the fellowship were told not to talk or fellowship with her. Devastated, Amber avoided church for a year, thinking that there must be something seriously wrong with her faith. Only after she became friends with a healthy believer did she begin to realize that her problem was her own lack of self-worth and understanding of spiritual authority. As her counselor, it was obvious to me that Attila the Hun had once again pillaged Doris Doormat, leaving devastation and confusion in his wake.

All of us function in some type of leadership. It may be in the area of parenting, church leadership, or as a supervisor on a job. Children even begin practicing leadership skills as they learn to take care of the family pet. Similarly, all of us must relate to those in authority in some regard. Unfortunately, when people have lived in a dysfunctional home or abnormal church, they may not be too sure what a healthy home or church looks like. Their unhealthy concepts of authority and submission carry over into their eternal associations.

One of the most frightening Scriptures in the Bible can be Hebrews 13:17, "Obey your leaders and submit to their authority. They keep watch over you as those who will give account" (NASB). Two things need to be recognized in this verse. First, leadership will someday have to give an account for how they lead those who follow them. Second, those who follow leaders are to obey and submit to those leaders.

God has intended that we each be related to a local church. Church is people—His people. We cannot become all that God desires without other people's individual touch upon our lives. It is in the midst of His people that we become mature and Christlike. Further, God particularly shapes us by placing leaders in our lives that have been given the responsibility to train and equip us in Christ. We are the richer and better for submitting ourselves to true spiritual authorities.

> It was he who gave some to be apostles, some to be prophets, some to be evangelists, and some to be pastors and teachers, to prepare God's people for works of service, so that the body of Christ may be built up until we all reach unity in the faith and in the knowledge of the Son of God and become mature, attaining to the whole measure of the fullness of

Christ. Then we will no longer be infants, tossed back and forth by the waves, and blown here and there by every wind of teaching and by the cunning and craftiness of men in their deceitful scheming (Ephesians 4:11-14 NIV).

Spiritual leadership

Dr. J. Robert Clinton states, "A spiritual leader is any person with the God-given capacity and God-given responsibility who is influencing a specific group of God's people toward God's purpose for that group."[iv] This is an excellent definition of spiritual leadership for two reasons: First, it is broad. Its scope includes husbands, elders, parents, pastors, and other godly leaders. Secondly, it accurately defines spiritual leaders. This separates spiritual leadership from other leadership models such as those seen in the world of business or politics.

The healthy leader has both a fear of God and a passionate desire to please Him in every way. In the leader's personal history, there are many dealings from God and lessons learned. This person knows that he will have to give an account to Jesus in days-not-too-future for his thoughts, words, and deeds as God's servant. Consequently, he is acutely aware of the lordship of Jesus Christ: It is His church, His people, His work, and His fame.

The New Testament always identifies the leaders of a local church as working together as a team. For example, in Philippians 1:1, the leadership is addressed as a plurality: the overseers and deacons. "Paul and Timothy, bond-servants of Christ Jesus, to all the saints in Christ Jesus who are in Philippi, including the overseers and deacons" (NASB). The burden of church direction, finances, and decision-making is much lighter if it is carried on many shoulders. Accountability is also afforded a leadership team because no one is acting independently with their own agenda. This applies to a husband and wife team as well as a church.

In addition, the New Testament places its emphasis upon a leader's character and not his gifting. Gifts and callings are important. However, maturity validates the gift and calling.

Note that all the qualifications required of men and women who would be leaders in God's church are character qualities and not gifts (see 1 Timothy 3). A person may be called to pastor, but it is maturity that determines the timing for him to wear the title of pastor or elder. Someone has well said, "If you were a donkey before you prophesied, then you will be one after you prophesy."

Foundational to those who would serve as leaders is their ability to relate to other people in a healthy way. Does the prospective leader actively love and care for people? What are the indications that he does? Some leaders tend to use people and need them to validate their ministry. Others leave a trail of broken relationships and wounded folks in their wake. Many neglect their marriage and family for the work of the ministry. Relational health is a must for anyone who will serve as a leader in God's church.

One of the tests for leadership we use in the church we pastor is to know a person long enough to have watched him or her in the midst of a trial. How does this person handle his relationships when under pressure? Does she know how to process offense and restore relationships? Does he know his weak areas and does he welcome accountability? Is she a good follower, and can she take correction as an opportunity to learn and grow? What is his style of confrontation, and is he the first to ask for forgiveness when needed? Does she handle the trial with scriptural integrity? Does he understand team ministry? Finally, is he seeking to rightly represent the Lord Jesus in the midst of this trial?

Evaluating authority

In relating to a person in a position of authority, it is helpful to understand the kind of authority they are wielding. People in leadership roles at any given time are exercising one of three kinds of authority. Not all have God's approval for use in His kingdom. During our years at L.I.F.E. Bible College, Don Pickerill taught on the subject of these three types of authority—*positional*, *earned*, and *demand* authority.

By *positional* authority, we are referring to people who are placed in positions of authority and given a title to designate that position. Although one may indeed have a title, or the positional authority of pastor, teacher, prophet, elder, or husband, this does not tell us if they are a leader or what kind of leader they are. Just because someone carries a title does not mean they also have spiritual authority. The title/position does not convey spiritual authority! In other words, it is the spiritual authority in a person that gives meaning to their title/position and not vice versa. It is the ideal that every person with a title or position also has spiritual authority, but this is not always the case.

The following titles indicate some of the most obvious examples of positional authority. *Parents* are given the position and responsibility of being authorities over their children. The Scriptures give many instructions to help them in this role (see Ephesians 6:4). *Husbands* are given a very limited authority over their wives. They are designated the head of the husband-wife relationship (Ephesians 5:23). Additionally, the husband is charged with responsibility for the care of the wife (see 1 Peter 3:7 & Ephesians 5:28-29).

Elders are given the responsibility or position of overseers for God's church by virtue of their age and proven character (see Acts 20:17, 28). The five-fold ministry offices of *apostles*, *prophets*, *evangelists*, *pastors*, and *teachers* are given positions and authority to build and equip Christ's church. Again, it is one thing to have a title, but it is quite another to deserve the title. In 1 Timothy 3:7-11, Paul reminds us that a leader must be worthy of respect (see also Titus 1:5-9). It is to be underscored that each of the above positions and titles has an attending function and responsibility. The title of *husband* is just a title if it is not attended with the husband's love for his wife. There is no true authority without responsibility.

In a very real sense, we must each earn the right and privilege of being God's delegated authority in another person's life. Title does not confer upon us that authority. In the kingdom, people aren't led against their will. People must give us permission to lead them as their elder, pastor, husband, or parent. So how do you become a leader that others follow? Or in referring back to our definition of spiritual authority, how does one develop credibility in the hearts of others so that they will follow our leading? And how does one gain the second type of authority—that of *earned* authority?

In Scripture, two qualities are repeatedly referred to that give us clues. First, the New Testament always points the would-be leader to servanthood (see Matthew 20:25-28; Mark 10:42-45; Luke 22:24-27). A servant in simplest terms is someone who makes life better for you. It is in serving others that we gain credibility in the hearts of people. When people perceive that we have their highest good in mind, they will follow our lead. Leadership is never to be separated from service. Jesus stressed that servanthood is the foundation from which all ministry flows. It was his final and most important message to his disciples, right before he left His entire ministry in their hands (see John 13). To neglect servanthood is to step outside the defining lines of genuine leadership.

Paul confirms this in his writings. He explains that the only legitimate use of authority is in serving others. "For we do not preach ourselves but Christ Jesus as Lord and ourselves your servants for Jesus' sake" (2 Corinthians 4:5 NIV). "Let a man regard us in this manner, as servants" (1 Corinthians 4:1 NASB).

Leaders are never simply *over* others in terms of titles, power, or positions. Instead, they are seen *among* people as servants. Both Paul and Peter are intentional in using the preposition "among" to describe the servanthood being lived out by leaders in the midst of God's people. "You know what kind of men we proved to be *among* you" (1 Thessalonians 1:5 NASB, *italics mine*). "Appreciate those who diligently labor *among* you" (1 Thessalonians 5:12 NASB, *italics mine*). "The elders who are *among* you I exhort . . . shepherd the flock of God which is *among* you" (1 Peter 5:1-2 NKJV, *italics mine*).

Earned authority always bases its existence in that of a servant and as an example to others. As true spiritual authority, it will manifest itself in a person having those characteristics that others want to emulate. In other words, this type of authority is followable. The New Testament states, "Show yourself an *example*" (1 Timothy 4:12 NASB, *italics mine*). "Being *examples* to the flock" (1 Peter 5:3 NIV, *italics mine*). "Be *imitators* of me, just as I also am of Christ" (1 Corinthians 11:1 NASB, *italics mine*). "Brethren, join in following my *example*, and observe those who walk according to the *pattern* you have in us" (Philippians 3:17 NASB, *italics mine*). (The word *example* can be translated from the Greek as "mimic.")

This does not mean the leader has to be perfect! However, he is making discernable headway in his growth in Christ. It is the life of example that gives substance to the titles and positions that may have been conferred upon us. These qualities alone give us the true ability to influence others.

The third way that authority is exercised is *demand* authority. Many who move in spiritual authority operate as dictators. Some may act like little Hitlers, but most are benevolent rulers. We often find these people functioning as pastors, church leaders, and husbands. They may have good hearts, but insecurities, wrong training, or misconceptions of biblical authority predetermine their dominating style of leadership.

Some leaders wield authority like it was a running chainsaw. Cutting down people, maiming followers, shredding people's dreams, and eroding trust, they bring dishonor to Jesus and harm to His people. Paul was very aware of this danger when he wrote, "For this reason I am writing these things while absent, in order that when present I may not use severity, in accordance with the authority which the Lord gave me, for building up and not for tearing down" (2 Corinthians 13:10 NASB).

Frustrated and misguided leaders often demand and threaten others in order to get their way. Invoking their title or position, they use authority illegitimately to achieve personal ends. Perhaps they have good intentions, such as doing an outreach for Christ or correcting an erring child's behavior, but the method used to attain such an end is sinful. For example, intimidating someone with rage or swearing to achieve Christian aims is unacceptable. So is inferring that someone who disagrees with leaders is in rebellion, when the person might only be stating his concerns and cautions.

Spiritual leaders can be susceptible to operating in this false authority. Paul reproves the church at Corinth for falling under the control of leaders wielding false authority, more befitting Attila the Hun than Christ the Lord. He warns, "In fact, you even put up with anyone who enslaves you or exploits you or takes advantage of you or pushes himself forward or slaps you in the face" (2 Corinthians 11:20 NIV). In other words, "Get a clue Corinthians; this guy is not a representative of Christ!"

John writes in the book of Revelation that people claiming to be spiritual leaders were, in fact, wielding false authority. Dominating and controlling God's people, John identifies them as Nicolaitans (see Revelation 2:6, 15). *Niko* is the Greek word for "dominion" and *lao* is the word for "people." Combined, the word *Nicolaitan* means "to conquer people."

Here are four helps to discern whether you or someone you know is the subject of unnatural control by a leader:

> *Emotional manipulation* occurs when a leader uses angry outbursts and verbal assaults to control people.

> *Spiritual manipulation* happens when a leader guides others through words from God, visions, or dreams that are actually his own personal agenda.

> *Abuse* occurs when a leader uses their position to harm another sexually, physically, mentally, spiritually, or verbally.

> *Psychological manipulation* is detected when a person makes sudden and drastic changes in their lifestyle or appearance. Cults are notorious for this style of manipulation. Members cut off all outside friendships, give all their savings to the cult, and often change their eating habits. I have counseled wives whose husbands used this form of control. We have refugees in our fellowship who were involved in churches that controlled their people in this manner.

So how do we relate to Genghis Khan and others who exercise *demand authority*? The following general guideline can help: Peter says it is better to obey God than man (see Acts 5:29). Therefore, submission to *demand authority*, that which would cause us to sin against our own conscience or God, is *never* an option. Learn to say the following word in love: "No!"

Relating to authority with submission

Webster's Dictionary defines *submit* as a verb meaning "to give over or yield to the power or authority of another." No word in the English language is more misunderstood than the word *submission*. Radical feminists reject the word outright. To them, it means the acknowledgement of woman's inferiority to man. To some Christian women, it is a term of abuse. They have been told by men and denominations alike to submit in the face of the most outrageous behaviors from husbands. Still on other fronts, submission is a word of control used by cults, and even Christian ministries, in order to have their will prevail over the behavior of their followers.

So, what does biblical submission really mean? In Ephesians 5:21, Paul states, "submit to one another out of reverence for Christ" (NIV). The Greek word for "submit" is *hupotassomenoi*. This word is best translated, "give way to one another." To "give" keeps this powerful word close to the idea of love. In John 3:16, we see love as the giving of Jesus by the Father to a needy world. Also, this definition is in keeping with 1 Corinthians 13:5, which tells us that love does not insist on its own way. Love places the needs and interests of others ahead of itself (see Philippians 2:3-4 and Romans 12:10).

When we divorce submission from the context of God's love, it becomes cruel, degrading, and repulsive. Separate it from the context of the Holy Spirit, and it becomes impossible. Interestingly, submission is the last of four manifestations of being filled with the Holy Spirit as seen in Ephesians 5:18-21.

In Ephesians 5:21, "Submit to one another out of reverence for Christ" (NIV), we see believers simply spoken of as *one another*. In saying this, all God's sons and daughters are placed on equal ground. All are equally loved and none afforded an inferior or superior status. And because all before God are equal, we will, as the situation calls for it, give way to one another regardless of one another's age, gender, gifting, spiritual maturity, or race (see Galatians 3:27-28).

We are simply brothers and sisters who are each equally valuable as children of our heavenly Father, and we are each equally responsible to give way to the other as love would dictate. At times, the brother (who is also a husband), will give way to his wife on matters where she has better insight and wisdom. And conversely, the wife (his sister in Christ) will do the same. And there will certainly be times when both parents will yield to the counsel and input of their children. Church leaders should often yield to the advice of their followers. It is only stubborn pride that would resist giving way to someone who has our best interest and highest good in mind.

> Submit to one another out of reverence for Christ. Wives, submit to your husbands as to the Lord. For the husband is the head of the wife as Christ is the head of the church, his body, of which he is the Savior (Ephesians 5:21-23 NIV).

Before the wife is addressed, Paul reminds the marriage partners that submission is a mutual activity. He then goes on to give reasons why the wife will find submission a way to honor her husband and the Lord. Here, Paul puts forth two reasons why a woman is to give way to her husband.

First, Paul states she is to give way to her husband as to the Lord. That is, her husband has been given certain limited authority over his own wife. If all God's people are of equal value before God, why, then, is the wife singled out as needing to submit? The answer is found in creation. It is of sovereign design that the man is designated the head of a marriage relationship. Paul states this purpose in other New Testament passages: God chose woman to be created after the man, out of the man, and for the man. However, both are equal and not to be independent of each other (see 1 Corinthians 11:3-12).

It is vital to remember that the emphasis here is order and not superiority. Submission means that a person is placing himself

105

or herself under the God-given authority of another. Or simply put, it is giving way to God-given authority in our lives. It means strength to us and not weakness. It is what made Jesus strong in His earthly walk. He submitted continually to the gracious will of God.

The second reason given for submission is incarnation. When a husband fully loves his wife like Christ loves the church, and when a wife fully gives way to this love, then the world sees Christ and His bride. Submitting one to another in a church arena is another way the world knows that our love is real—they can see a picture that is able to profoundly impact them (see John 13:34-35; John 17:21, 23; Ephesians 5:24-32). Further, it must be noted that a person's submission is a voluntary, joyful, and free act of worship as unto the Lord. It is never something that can be demanded of her by an irate mate or church leader.

Submission does not signify that a person is to be a doormat. A clear picture of this is seen in Acts 5:1-11. A husband named Ananias tried to deceive God's church and was immediately judged. He fell over dead. Afterwards, his wife, Sapphira, was asked, "Did you submit to your husband and go along with his plan?" And because she did submit rather than challenge him, she was also condemned. She, too, fell over dead.

It is an error to equate submission with mindless obedience to an authority's every wish or demand. Sapphira's error brought severe consequences. Submitting to and obeying those who have authority over us is commendable, as long as those God-given authorities are walking in obedience to Scripture. When authorities err, Scripture never allows for a passive ignoring of the problem. Matthew 18 is clear: I must go to my sinning brother and correct him, even if he is my husband or pastor!

The following are several signs of counterfeit submission present in the dysfunctional husband-wife relationship or between a pastor and his congregation.

> *Unnatural submission* is seen when, under the guise of caring for a person's welfare, her free will is severely stifled or taken away. It is counterfeit submission if an individual

106

loses her ability to follow her own conscience on a matter or to make her own daily decisions. Examples are when a husband requires total accountability for every cent spent by a wife or a detailed accounting of her personal activities.

➤ *Abuse* takes place when a leader in the home or church does not lead out of love, but rather from threats, demands, and, therefore, fear. Abuse is always the illegitimate use of authority, which hurts and degrades others sexually, physically, emotionally, or spiritually.

➤ *Repressed communication* happens when an individual is not allowed to hold an opposing opinion to that of his authority.

➤ *False guilt* results when regular criticism, ridicule, and blame cause a person to be left with little sense of worth.

➤ *Denial* is evident when an individual may deny that there is anything wrong in the marriage or church. Submission is interpreted as doing whatever it takes to keep peace.

Leadership that loves as Christ loves and leads His church will do whatever is needed to see people fully equipped and released into their gifts and calling. And certainly, the husband, as head of the husband/wife relationship, is to be his wife's covering (see Ruth 3:9). Church leaders are also to act as coverings for their congregation. But make no mistake: "Covering" is a term of protection and blessing. We ensure the protection of whatever is precious to us. Covering is not the same as "lid." A lid, by definition, squelches and holds down things and people. This is not how Jesus, the head of the church, acts toward His bride.

Chapter application:

1. Can people have gifts without character in their lives? Why or why not?

2. Do you think most churches model a plurality of leaders or a single leader at the top? Why might this be dangerous?

3. How have you seen those operating in authority serve *among* the people they lead?

4. What makes some leaders so controlling?

5. Who has been the best representative of a spiritual authority in your life and why?

6. Describe the last time you submitted to another brother or sister over an issue?

Part Three

It's All About Us!

Chapter 11
Rules and Tools for Kingdom Communication

God is a communicator! He is always speaking. In fact, one of His names is Word of God. Words are important to God, as are other forms of communication. He loves music, dance, and art. He reads our hearts like you and I might read a book.

Relationships begin and are sustained through communication, whether spoken or non-spoken. Our relationship with God is no exception. He has never stopped communicating and seeking to connect with us. As kingdom people, He expects us to seek interaction and connectedness with one another.

> Then those who feared the LORD talked with each other, and the LORD listened and heard. A scroll of remembrance was written in his presence concerning those who feared the LORD and honored his name (Malachi 3:16 NIV).

Apparently, whom we talk to, what we talk about, and how we talk about it reveals much about our fear of the Lord. In fact, God seems to be taking notes! He eavesdrops on our conversations and has one of His angel scribes write down the things we say that reveal our honor and fear of Him. One wonders what He intends to do with this book of remembrance. I also wonder what He is doing with the things we say that display our lack of honor and fear of His name!

111

Boundaries of communication

How we communicate with one another is important to God. Our tone of voice, our words, our silence, the way we use body language, and even the choice of subjects are all addressed in Scripture. There are some forms and subjects of communication that are off limits to believers, and others that are encouraged as right and good.

> There are six things which the LORD hates, yes, seven which are an abomination to Him: Haughty eyes, a lying tongue, and hands that shed innocent blood, A heart that devises wicked plans, feet that run rapidly to evil, A false witness [who] utters lies, and one who spreads strife among brothers (Proverbs 6:16-19 NASB).

Each of these seven things are verbal or non-verbal forms of communication. They represent the communication of the kingdom of darkness. I find it interesting that those who call on the Lord often take some of these abominations very lightly when they should be regarded as outside the boundary lines of godly communication.

Boundary lines provide a secure place of safety, much as the "Danger, Do Not Enter" signs at Disneyland provide safety to all who would enjoy the various rides at Disneyland's Magic Kingdom. These unobtrusive warnings are placed in strategic locations near each ride to keep visitors away from the section of dangerous machinery operating the ride. As citizens of a new kingdom, we have to learn the language of communication that will be ours for the rest of eternity. The following boundary lines, or rules, are given in Scripture for our protection.

Why we are to communicate—The italicized words in the following verses explain godly motives for communication:

➤ "Let your conversation be always full of grace, seasoned with salt, *so that you may know how to answer everyone*" (Colossians 4:6 NIV, *italics mine*).

➤ "In all things show yourself to be . . . sound [in] speech which is beyond reproach, *in order that the opponent may be put to shame, having nothing bad to say about us"* (Titus 2:7-8 NASB, *italics mine*).

➢ "Having many things to write to you, I do not want to [do so] with paper and ink; but I hope to come to you and speak face to face, *that your joy may be made full"* (2 John 1:12 NASB, *italics mine*).

➢ *"But I tell you that men will have to give account on the day of judgment for every careless word they have spoken. For by your words you will be acquitted, and by your words you will be condemned"* (Matthew 12:36-37 NIV, *italics mine*).

➢ "The wise in heart are called discerning, and pleasant words promote instruction. Understanding is a fountain of life to those who have it, but folly brings punishment to fools. A wise man's heart guides his mouth, and his lips promote instruction. *Pleasant words are a honeycomb, sweet to the soul and healing to the bones"* (Proverbs 16:21-24 NIV, *italics mine*).

What we are to communicate—The italicized words in the following verses suggest topics for godly communication:

➢ "Love the LORD your God with all your heart and with all your soul and with all your strength. *These commandments that I give you today are to be upon your hearts.* Impress them on your children. Talk about them when you sit at home and when you walk along the road, when you lie down and when you get up" (Deuteronomy 6:5-7 NIV, *italics mine*).

➢ *"Pleasant words* are a honeycomb, sweet to the soul and healing to the bones" (Proverbs 16:24 NIV, *italics mine*).

➢ "The tongue of the wise commends *knowledge*, but the mouth of the fool gushes folly" (Proverbs 15: 2 NIV, *italics mine*).

➢ "To sum up, let all be harmonious, sympathetic, brotherly, kindhearted, and humble in spirit; not returning evil for evil, or insult for insult, but giving a blessing instead . . . *always [being] ready to make a defense to everyone who asks you to give an account for the hope that is in you"* (1 Peter 3:8-9, 15 NASB, *italics mine*).

How we are to communicate—The italicized words in the following verses set the tone or flavor of godly communication:

➢ *"Let your conversation be always full of grace, seasoned with salt,* so that you may know how to answer everyone" (Colossians 4:6 NIV, *italics mine).*

➢ *"In all things show yourself to be...sound [in] speech which is beyond reproach"* (Titus 2:7-8 NASB, *italics mine*).

➢ "But let everyone be *quick to hear, slow to speak [and] slow to anger"* (James 1:19 NASB, *italics mine*).

➢ *"He who answers before listening—that is his folly and his shame"* (Proverbs 18:13 NIV, *italics mine*).

➢ *"May the words of my mouth and the meditation of my heart be pleasing in your sight,* O LORD, my Rock and my Redeemer" (Psalm 19:14 NIV, *italics mine*).

➢ "The wise in heart are called discerning, and pleasant words promote instruction. *A wise man's heart guides his mouth, and his lips promote instruction"* (Proverbs 16:21, 23 NIV, *italics mine*).

➢ *"A man of knowledge uses words with restraint, and a man of understanding is even-tempered.* Even a fool is thought wise if he keeps silent, and discerning if he holds his tongue" (Proverbs 17:27, 28 NIV, *italics mine*).

➢ "A man who lacks judgment derides his neighbor, *but a man of understanding holds his tongue.* A gossip betrays a confidence, but *a trustworthy man keeps a secret"* (Proverbs 11:12-13 NIV, *italics mine*).

➢ *"A gentle answer turns away wrath, but a harsh word stirs up anger. The tongue of the wise commends knowledge,* but the mouth of the fool gushes folly" (Proverbs 15:1-2 NIV, *italics mine*).

➢ "To sum up, *let all be harmonious, sympathetic, brotherly, kindhearted, and humble in spirit; not returning evil for evil, or insult for insult, but giving a blessing instead*; for you were called for the very purpose that you might inherit a blessing. For, 'Let him who means to love life and see good days refrain his tongue from evil and his lips from speaking guile. *'And let him turn away from evil and do good; let him seek peace and pursue it . . .'* always [being] ready to make a defense to everyone who asks you to give an account for the hope that is in you, *yet with gentleness and reverence"* (1 Peter 3:8-11, 15 NASB, *italics mine*).

What we are to avoid in communication—The italicized words in the following verses detail what are unacceptable forms of communication:

➢ "Remind the people to be subject to rulers and authorities . . . *to slander no one*, to be peaceable and considerate, and to show true humility toward all men" (Titus 3:1-2 NIV, *italics mine*).

➢ *"Get rid of all bitterness, rage and anger, brawling and slander, along with every form of malice"* (Ephesians 4:31 NIV, *italics mine*).

➢ *"But now you also, put them all aside: anger, wrath, malice, slander, [and] abusive speech from your mouth"* (Colossians 3:8 NASB, *italics mine*).

➢ "Therefore, laying aside all malice, all guile, hypocrisy, envy, and all *evil speaking"* (1 Peter 2:1 NKJ, *italics mine*).

➢ *"But the things that come out of the mouth come from the heart, and these make a man 'unclean.' For out of the heart come evil thoughts, murder, adultery, sexual immorality, theft, false testimony, slander"* (Matthew 15:18-19 NIV, *italics mine*).

➢ "Above all, my brothers, *do not swear*—not by heaven or by earth or by anything else. Let your "Yes" be yes, and your "No," no, or you will be condemned" (James 5:12 NIV, *italics mine*).

➢ "You have heard that the ancients were told, 'You shall not commit murder' and 'Whoever commits murder shall be liable to the court.' But I say to you that *everyone who is angry with his brother shall be guilty before the court; and whoever shall say to his brother, 'Raca,' shall be guilty before the supreme court; and whoever shall say, 'You fool,' shall be guilty [enough to go] into the fiery hell"* (Matthew 5:21-22 NASB, *italics mine*).

➢ "Remind [them] of these things, and solemnly charge [them] in the presence of God *not to wrangle about words, which is useless, [and leads] to the ruin of the hearers.* Be diligent to present yourself approved to God as a workman who does not need to be ashamed, handling accurately the word of truth. *But avoid worldly [and] empty chatter, for it will lead to further ungodliness, and their talk will spread like gangrene"* (2 Timothy 2:14-17 NASB, *italics mine*).

➢ "*. . . not returning evil for evil, or insult for insult . . .* For, 'Let him who means to love life and see good days *Refrain his tongue from evil and his lips from speaking guile.'* And let him turn away from evil and do good; let him seek peace and pursue it'" (1 Peter 3:9-11 NASB, *italics mine*).

➢ "*If anyone considers himself religious and yet does not keep a tight rein on his tongue, he deceives himself and his religion is worthless"* (James 1:26 NIV, *italics mine*).

Learning the language of the opposite sex

Besides learning the rules of communication, we also need to understand the language of the opposite sex. Half of the people that live on this planet are wired differently than ourselves. For example, a mother attempts a meaningful conversation with a son who interprets her effort as invading his space. A daughter feels her father doesn't have time to listen to her innermost thoughts while the dad thinks he is doing pretty well to listen to her during halftime of the football game. A man interprets a woman employer as bossy and domineering, when she sees herself as confidently overseeing the details of the business. A male soccer coach wants to take his young team to view a professional soccer game, yet he has to convince a soccer mom that the trip will be safe and they will be home on time. She apparently has a funny feeling about the security of the trip. He thinks she's nuts.

Most of the communication problems that arise between men and women have to do with not understanding the basic differences between male and female. A man keeps expecting a woman to think like him, act like him, and respond like he does. Of course, she is not a man so she will not think, act, or respond like he is expecting. The same goes for a woman's expectations of a man. She expects him to think like a woman. Understanding our differences is a basic tool of communication.

Men are single-minded. They think about one thing at a time. At some point between the 16th and 26th weeks of gestational development, a boy baby is washed with a testosterone bath. This bath brings out the masculine traits in the child and severs some of the nerve endings between the right and left hemispheres of his brain. This means that a male does not switch between the functions of the two sides of his brain very quickly. This allows him to focus intently on one thing at a time and be very good at what he is doing. However, he will find it difficult to do two things at once—such as talk on the phone with a friend *and* listen to his wife's comments.

On the other hand, a woman has no problem doing multiple tasks at the same time. She did not have the testosterone bath, and can easily use both sides of her brain at once. She can plan a week's menu in her imagination, help the kids with their homework, and cook dinner all at one time. However, this can be a problem when her husband needs her full attention, such as during their intimate times together.

This is why a woman should never try to have a serious, deep conversation with a man while he is focused on something else—like driving the car. Usually, he will have very little memory of the details of the conversation as the driving is consuming his attention. If he does give her his concentrated attention, he will probably miss their turnoff or nearly hit another car. Either way, she will feel like he is not listening to her and is rejecting her need for an important discussion. Actually, he is just doing his job as a man—concentrating on the one thing he is currently doing. My daughter has learned to avoid serious discussions with her dad when he is driving—too many near accidents!

Men are also competitors. For a man, courtship is a competition that he wants to win. Once the wedding is over, so is the work of winning his bride. "I do" means "I'm done." He has won and the contest is over. In truth, the work of winning her heart has just begun. On the other hand, women are nurturers. She is just getting into her element when the wedding is over. She will nurture her husband, her children, and her marriage.

Unfortunately, these differences work against each other. A woman resents her husband when he no longer seems to care about her—he is no longer putting anything emotionally into the marriage. Yes, he is working and bringing home a paycheck, but work is just another focus for his competitive nature and she does not view that contribution as nurturing the emotional needs of the marriage. Often, he will spend an evening a week with his buddies and neglect to set a regular weekly date night with her. Over time, a woman will become bitter and distant because her man does not recognize the need to continually court her.

The men on a church committee may be more inclined to tackle a project and get on to the next one as soon as the first is completed. Once they have conquered, they want another challenge. The women on the committee will linger over the parts of the project that need attention and will voice concern over how the process is affecting the members of the church. They are nurturing the project. Both perspectives are needed to have a balanced committee!

Similarly, men are solution-oriented while a woman focuses on the journey. A man enters a conversation looking for a solution. A woman enters a conversation to process something—she may not at all be interested in a solution. This makes for frustration as a man may not feel a need for conversation or, when he does allow his wife or daughter time to talk, he will jump to give solutions. He gets frustrated with her need to talk over and over again about something. On the other hand, his wife will resent his lack of caring about the journey of discussion and listening to her as she processes her problems.

As pastors, we see this same irritation operating between the men and women at church. The women process problems through conversation. The men process problems by mental deliberation and then presenting their solution. When men understand that women process through talk, or thinking out loud, they are more likely to be patient when working with them.

Unspoken rules

All of us have unspoken rules that guide the way we live our lives. These rules can be conscious or unconscious. They can be positive or negative. However, conflict usually happens when someone breaks one of our unspoken rules. The offender is confused because he doesn't understand the basis for our anger. For example, in my family of origin, it was always my dad who locked up the house at night. In Tom's family of origin, his mother always locked the doors and turned off the lights. Conflict arose because we each had an expectation concerning who would secure the home each night. I had an unspoken rule that my husband was supposed to lock the doors and switch off the lights. His unspoken rule dictated that I do it.

If you are married, you were probably faced with a decision of how to celebrate Christmas. When would the presents get opened? How would you spend Christmas Eve or Christmas morning? Based on how you were raised, you both had certain expectations. Unless you decided together how Christmas was going to be spent, you probably went through a lot of inner turmoil and frustration over your unspoken rules being transgressed.

We bring many unspoken rules into our marriage and we also develop new rules after the honeymoon. This is fine when the unspoken rule becomes spoken and acknowledged by both as acceptable. But when an unspoken rule remains unspoken and is not shared by both parties, then it can cause confusion, frustration, and conflict.

Unspoken rules can also cause problems in a church setting. For example, some people who have become part of our church financial council thought it would function like the church board from their previous church. They automatically began to make decisions that were the responsibility of our eldership or denominational authorities. This caused confusion and conflict.

Here are some examples of unspoken rules that we have encountered: Always eat dinner together as a family. Never get in debt. Make your bed when you get out of it in the morning. Don't talk about your feelings. A woman cleans the house and the man brings home the paycheck. Never leave dirty clothes on the floor. Women change diapers. When money arrives unexpectedly, we use it to pay off debts. When money arrives unexpectedly, we use it for recreation. Never disagree with the pastor. Sunday service should be one hour long.

Learning to listen

Learning to communicate involves listening to what the other person is attempting to convey. This can be difficult if there is tension between you and another. However, love will always seek to really see something from another's perspective. This doesn't mean you have to agree with them, but if you don't really hear what they are saying, then you can't really respond properly. Following are three comments and questions to use when you are trying to hear and interpret what another is communicating (Remember to say them with a nice tone of voice!):

"Why do you think that?"

"Explain it from another angle, please, so I can be sure I am really catching all that you want me to hear."

"This is what I think you are saying. Correct me if I have it wrong." (Then repeat back to the person what you think they said.)

Constructive confrontations

Confrontation is unavoidable in kingdom living. However, most of us avoid it at all costs because it is so uncomfortable. When required to confront we often make a mess of things and determine never to do it again! This conclusion only leads to future frustration, which leads again to wrong ways of confronting situations needing attention. Somehow, we have to learn that confrontation is one of God's ways of encouraging people to grow—including us!

You know by the way you feel after a confrontation if the communication has been uplifting and helpful. If you feel bad, then you feel criticized. If you feel good, then you have been encouraged and strengthened to grow and change. There are ways to address concerns with graciousness without adding criticism. Encouragement coupled with wisdom will always find a way to help another see a blind spot and overcome it.

A healthy practice is to evaluate all the times that someone has confronted you about needed change. Make a list of what was positive about the confrontation and could be added to your toolbox of confrontational strategies. Then make a list of what was negative about the confrontation and determine never to do the same thing in any of your times of confronting others.

Chapter application

Choose a recent conversation that did not go well for you. Use the following worksheet to examine the conversation and learn from the experience. You will find the Scriptures presented in this chapter helpful in completing the exercise. By repeatedly using this worksheet in a communication journal, you will find your relationships improving.

Godly Communication Worksheet:

1. Describe the conversation/situation:

2. "Love will always seek to really see something from another's perspective." What was the person trying to convey to me? How do I know?

3. What words did I use to show that I was really listening?

4. What type of body language did I use to put the person at ease in our conversation?

5. What Scriptures demonstrate that I represented the Lord Jesus correctly in this conversation? (Cite and explain biblical references.)

6. What mistakes did I make in this conversation? (Cite and explain biblical references.)

Chapter 12

Forever Friends

Christy, Vickie, Paula, and I have known each other for over 25 years. We laughed together as our babies learned to toddle, prayed our teens into adulthood, and are now watching our children marry and bring our adorable grandchildren into existence. We encourage each other's strengths and tolerate the quirks. Our lives are busy and complicated. Still, we manage to set aside the second Friday of each month for lunch and catching up on all the news. We intend to keep this monthly date for at least the next millennium or two.

People are eternal. And, if they are kingdom people, then our relationship with them will be unending We have before us many eons of time to get to know each believer in a deep and meaningful way. This includes those we interact with now and those we don't yet know. Here on Earth, though, we are limited in how much we can get to know the relatively few people with whom we associate.

As God, Jesus knows each of us individually and intimately. However, when He walked on Earth he was restricted in how many close friends He had. His *closest* friend was John. His *intimate* circle of friends was only three—Peter, James, and John. The rest of the twelve, along with a few others such as Mary, Martha, and their brother, made up his close circle of *good* friends. Those recognized as the "70" could be called His *general* group of friends. The large group of 500 that were known to follow Him would be considered *acquaintances*.

We usually see this same pattern in our own relationships. Not everyone can be a best friend, nor will we have more then three or four intimate friends. Many will be our good friends and more will be our general group of associates. Even greater will be our acquaintances. This is normal and it often fluctuates at different points in our life journey. People come and go in this life, but, as much as possible, we want to keep each as a lifelong relationship, even if they no longer live near us. Our connection with each other reaches beyond this life and into eternity future.

One of the saddest times in the life of a pastor is to conduct a funeral for someone who has had very few friends and acquaintances. Unless the deceased is the last one living of his many friends, the lack of guests speaks volumes about his life. The greatest joy is to see crowds gather at a funeral to say goodbye to an old friend. The memories shared and the anticipation of a future reunion says much about the type of friend and associate the person was. Those who know that lifelong associations may also be eternal relationships will endeavor to invest themselves in the life of another, whether it is as a casual acquaintance or as a close friend.

Most of us become Christians without realizing that we are going to have to make changes in the way we relate to others. We are just so aglow with that first blush of knowing Jesus that little else matters. Sometimes people continue their whole Christian life without making the transition from old nature behavior to kingdom habits. It just never occurs to them that when the Bible gives instructions for relationships, they are expected to adjust themselves accordingly! How we treat each other is not an option in the kingdom of God, nor is it left to our opinion.

Transitioning from old ways of interacting to God's ways is not automatic or easy. However, once we know what God expects of us, we can make a choice to obey His instructions. At that point, the Holy Spirit gives us the power we need to turn instructions into life experiences. We don't have to do this in our own power or abilities! God is more committed to this process then we are, and it is He who is constantly giving us opportunities to obey Him.

Practicing the "one anothers"

One of the places we learn about kingdom friendships is in the "one anothers" of Scripture. The one anothers help define how we are to interact in the kingdom. In over 28 years of pastoring the same church, these one anothers have been the glue that has held our congregation together. If one reads them just as beautiful sayings or as one would read poetry, then some of the spiritual weight is drained from their importance. Following are just a few. What would each of them look like in your life if you started practicing them today?

➢ "A new commandment I give to you, that you *love one another*, even as I have loved you, that you also *love one another*. By this all men will know that you are My disciples, if you *have love for one another*" (John 13:34-35 NASB, *italics mine*).

➢ "Be *devoted to one another* in brotherly love; *give preference to one another* in honor" (Romans 12:10 NASB, *italics mine*).

➢ "Wherefore, *accept one another*, just as Christ also accepted us to the glory of God" (Romans 15:7 NASB, *italics mine*).

➢ "And concerning you, my brethren, I myself also am convinced that you yourselves are full of goodness, filled with all knowledge, and able also to *admonish one another*" (Romans 15:14 NASB, *italics mine*).

➢ "For you were called to freedom, brethren; only [do] not [turn] your freedom into an opportunity for the flesh, but through love *serve one another*" (Galatians 5:13 NASB, *italics mine*).

➢ ". . . with all humility and gentleness, with patience, *showing forbearance to one another in love*" (Ephesians 4:2 NASB, *italics mine*).

➢ "*bearing with one another, and forgiving each other*, whoever has a complaint against anyone; just as the Lord forgave you, so also should you" (Colossians 3:13 NASB, *italics mine*).

➢ "Therefore *comfort one another* with these words" (1 Thessalonians 4:18 NASB, *italics mine*).

➢ "Therefore *encourage one another,* and *build up one another,* just as you also are doing" (1 Thessalonians 5:11 NASB, *italics mine*).

➢ "But *encourage one another* day after day, as long as it is [still] called 'Today,' lest any one of you be hardened by the deceitfulness of sin" (Hebrews 3:13 NASB, *italics mine*).

➢ "Let us consider how to *stimulate one another to love and good deeds,* not forsaking our own assembling together, as is the habit of some, but *encouraging [one another]* and all the more, as you see the day drawing near" (Hebrews 10:24-25 NASB, *italics mine*).

➢ "*Greet one another* with a kiss of love. Peace be to you all who are in Christ" (1 Peter 5:14 NASB, *italics mine*).

Our oldest daughter's outdoor wedding was planned for 1:00 p.m. on an April afternoon. The day looked promising. But by 11:00 a.m. it was obvious that rain was on the way. Frantic calls were made to friends in our church and by 11:30 a.m. an army had arrived to move all of the outdoor decorations, chairs, and ceremony, indoors. Mary walked down the aisle right on time with over 400 people witnessing her vows and straining to hear her father's message. He was so nervous he forgot to turn on his microphone! These people had practiced the one anothers for so many years alongside us that nobody thought twice about rescuing a rain-threatened wedding.

How do we get friends?

Practicing the one anothers of Scripture is a sure way to have lots of friends. One more is the old Scottish proverb, "Keep good company and you will be counted one of them." Following are additional avenues for making friends:

Be friendly: "A man who has friends must himself be friendly, but there is a friend who sticks closer than a brother" (Proverbs 18:24 NKJV).

Keep your heart pure and your speech gracious: "He who loves a pure heart and whose speech is gracious will have the king for his friend" (Proverbs 22:11 NIV).

What qualities are to be in our friends?

Ralph Waldo Emerson said, "It is one of the blessings of old friends that you can afford to be stupid with them." True friends overlook failures and mistakes and seek to help one another grow. Other qualities to look for in friends are given in Scripture:

The desire to please God: "When a man's ways are pleasing to the LORD, he makes even his enemies live at peace with him" (Proverbs 16:7 NIV).

Faithfulness: "A friend loves at all times, and a brother is born for adversity" (Proverbs 17:17 NIV).

Understanding: "The purposes of a man's heart are deep waters, but a man of understanding draws them out" (Proverbs 20:5 NIV).

Wisdom and truthfulness: "A word aptly spoken is like apples of gold in settings of silver. Like an earring of gold or an ornament of fine gold is a wise man's rebuke to a listening ear" (Proverbs 25:11-12 NIV).

Self-control: "A fool gives full vent to his anger, but a wise man keeps himself under control" (Proverbs 29:11 NIV).

A pure heart: "Flee the evil desires of youth, and pursue righteousness, faith, love and peace, along with those who call on the Lord out of a pure heart" (2 Timothy 2:22 NIV).

What responsibilities does friendship involve?

Someone once said, "To have a good friend is one of the highest delights of life; to be a good friend is one of the noblest and most difficult undertakings." Friendships take work, but the rewards are eternal. Below are responsibilities of friendship:

Forgiveness: "Hatred stirs up dissension, but love covers over all wrongs" (Proverbs 10:12 NIV).

Confidentiality: "A gossip betrays a confidence, but a trustworthy man keeps a secret" (Proverbs 11:13 NIV). "If you argue your case with a neighbor, do not betray another man's confidence, or he who hears it may shame you and you will never lose your bad reputation" (Proverbs 25:9-10 NIV).

Kind words: "An anxious heart weighs a man down, but a kind word cheers him up" (Proverbs 12:25 NIV).

Accountability: "Wounds from a friend can be trusted, but an enemy multiplies kisses" (Proverbs 27:6 NIV). "As iron sharpens iron, so one man sharpens another" (Proverbs 27:17 NIV).

Wise counsel and faithfulness: "Perfume and incense bring joy to the heart, and the pleasantness of one's friend springs from his earnest counsel. Do not forsake your friend and the friend of your father, and do not go to your brother's house when disaster strikes you—better a neighbor nearby than a brother far away" (Proverbs 27:9-10 NIV).

Representation: "So Jesus went with them. He was not far from the house when *the centurion sent friends* to say to him: 'Lord, don't trouble yourself, for I do not deserve to have you come under my roof' " (Luke 7:6 NIV, *italics mine*).

Empathy: "And when she finds it, she calls her friends and neighbors together and says, 'Rejoice with me; I have found my lost coin.' " (Luke 15:9 NIV).

Provision: "The next day we landed at Sidon; and Julius, in kindness to Paul, allowed him to go to his friends so they might provide for his needs" (Acts 27:3 NIV).

Love: "Owe no one anything except to love one another, for he who loves another has fulfilled the law" (Romans 13:8 NKJV).

What are we to avoid in friendships?

A French proverb reveals, "Tell me who you frequent and I'll tell you who you are." God has opinions about what is acceptable and what is not in friendships. Below are things we are to steer clear of:

Talking too much: "When words are many, sin is not absent, but he who holds his tongue is wise" (Proverbs 10:19 NIV).

Dirty language or jokes: "The lips of the righteous know what is fitting, but the mouth of the wicked only what is perverse" (Proverbs 10:32 NIV).

Putting people down: "A man who lacks judgment derides his neighbor, but a man of understanding holds his tongue" (Proverbs 11:12 NIV).

Deception and gossip: "A perverse man stirs up dissension, and a gossip separates close friends" (Proverbs 16:28 NIV). "A gossip betrays a confidence; so avoid a man who talks too much" (Proverbs 20:19 NIV).

Not listening: "He who answers before listening—that is his folly and his shame" (Proverbs 18:13 NIV).

Flattery: "Many curry favor with a ruler, and everyone is the friend of a man who gives gifts" (Proverbs 19:6 NIV).

People who have anger issues: "Do not make friends with a hot-tempered man, do not associate with one easily angered, or you may learn his ways and get yourself ensnared" (Proverbs 22:24-25 NIV).

Ignoring personal boundaries, lying, unfaithfulness, and lack of discretion: "Seldom set foot in your neighbor's house—too much of you, and he will hate you. Like a club or a sword or a sharp arrow is the man who gives false testimony against his neighbor. Like a bad tooth or a lame foot is reliance on the unfaithful in times of trouble. Like one who takes away a garment on a cold day, or like vinegar poured on soda, is one who sings songs to a heavy heart" (Proverbs 25:17-20 NIV).

People who are sexually immoral, greedy, idolaters, slanders, drunks, or swindlers: "But now I am writing you that you must not associate with anyone who calls himself a brother but is sexually immoral or greedy, an idolater or a slanderer, a drunkard or a swindler. With such a man do not even eat" (1 Corinthians 5:11 NIV).

In conclusion, we find a wonderful overview in Zechariah 8:16-17 of how to relate to anyone who might be considered our neighbor: "These are the things that ye shall do; Speak ye every man the truth to his neighbor; execute the judgment of truth and peace in your gates: And let none of you imagine evil in your hearts against his neighbor; and love no false oath: for all these are things that I hate, saith the LORD" (KJV).

These instructions were very helpful when one neighbor threatened to sue us over a property line dispute. Our conversations with him were always sincere and cushioned in peace. The man eventually moved away, but because we kept our attitude right and continued to seek to represent Jesus to him, he remained a friend.

Chapter application:

1. Which of the instructions do you currently practice under the section, *How do we get friends?* What new instructions do you plan to put into practice?

2. Which of the instructions do you currently practice under the section, *What qualities are to be in our friends?* What new instructions do you plan to put into practice?

3. Which of the instructions do you currently practice under the section, *What responsibilities does friendship involve?* What new instructions do you plan to put into practice?

4. Which of the instructions do you currently practice under the section, *What are we to avoid in friendships?* What new instructions do you plan to put into practice?

Chapter 13

Walking Through the Hard Times

"Pastor, please come. Fred is so angry he just broke the lamp in a fit of rage." The message on the answering machine sounded desperate. Fred had been out of work for over three months. He roller-coastered between outbursts of anger and slumps of depression. His wife, Jenny, was becoming frustrated and didn't know what to do anymore. Eventually, Fred learned to deal with his anger and finally found another job. He now calls those days his dark period. Jenny calls them Hell. Looking back, Fred and Jenny are thankful they had the support of their church family as they walked through a difficult time in their lives. Their marriage survived and their love deepened.

Just as it is impossible to know the strength of a bridge until it is tested with the weight of a large truck, so we usually don't know the strength of our relationships until they are tested by adversity. Too often, friends and church members feel uncomfortable dealing with trauma or grief, and neglect the one going through a very difficult time.

How to relate to challenging people

Not every relationship is easy. Sometimes, those whom we are close to, go through difficult times that try our patience. They could be going through a divorce, a job loss, or perhaps a serious illness. Whatever the situation, it brings tension to our relationships. Other times, we are the ones who act in immature ways and try the patience of our family, friends, and acquaintances. Imperfect people do imperfect things. However, we aren't to give up on each other!

When people go through trying times, they need us to be there for them. How we are to relate during these times depends on the condition of the person. Is the person weak or discouraged? Are they in rebellion toward God or another? First Thessalonians 5:14-15 addresses this challenge: "And we urge you, brethren, admonish the unruly, encourage the fainthearted, help the weak, be patient with all men. See that no one repays another with evil for evil, but always seek after that which is good for one another and for all men" (NASB).

Patience is the umbrella of protection in relationships. Patience does not mean "to put up with," but to undergird or support one another for a long period of time. The above Scripture instructs us to be patient with all men, but especially four different types of people: the unruly, the fainthearted, the weak, and those who do evil to us. I'm sure you have met all four types.

The first is the person who is *unruly*. The Greek translation describes this person as out of line; having left their post; not keeping order or rank; insubordinate; disorderly; unable to be ruled, or a loafer. Most of us have behaved this way at some time or another—at least our parents would give testimony to such. Many adults still act unruly. According to 1 Thessalonians 5:14-15 our response to an unruly person is to admonish them or warn and instruct them. This reprimand must be undergirded with goodness, knowledge, and wisdom, and it must be based on the Word of God.

> "And concerning you, my brethren, I myself also am convinced that you yourselves are full of goodness, filled with all knowledge, and able also to admonish one another" (Romans 15:14 NASB). "Let the word of Christ richly dwell within you, with all wisdom teaching and admonishing one another with psalms [and] hymns [and] spiritual songs, singing with thankfulness in your hearts to God" (Colossians 3:16 NASB).

The second type of person who needs our patience is the one who is timid or *fainthearted*. The Greek describes this person as "small souled" or immature in the areas of his thoughts, emotions, and will. We all know people who are shy, fearful, or who haven't matured in certain areas of their thoughts and feelings. We are asked to encourage, or soothe and console such a person. To encourage someone means to impart courage to him. According to Vine's Expository Dictionary, we are to "stimulate them to the earnest discharge of the ordinary duties of life and to speak closely to them with tenderness." All this is to be done over a long period of time.

The third type of person needing patience is the one who is *weak and weary*. Those lacking strength need our support and help. They need us to hold on to them firmly. This is often the person who is ill or depressed.

The *one who does evil* against us is the fourth type of person who needs our patience. We are instructed to show him kindness and to seek after that which is good for him. This is often hard because we don't always know what is good for a person doing evil. However, if we remember that what we do represents God's love, than our response is usually clear. Our dilemma with our neighbor over a boundary dispute, mentioned in the last chapter, is a good example of how to respond to someone who is doing evil toward you.

The family: God's avenue for meeting needs

When Dave's mother's diabetes became too advanced for her to handle alone, she moved in with Dave and Vickie. The next two years were difficult for Vickie, as Dave worked out of town and wasn't home much. His mother was extremely demanding and selfish. We often wondered if Vickie's health would hold up to the stress of caring for such a negative and severe patient. Still, Dave and Vickie persevered in their commitment because of their love for her and faithfulness to the Lord. They grieved when she died.

A family is the smallest, yet most basic, unit of the church. One place Scripture clearly teaches this principle is in caring for believers who are in need. The Bible limits the role of the corporate church and state in this area. The emphasis of Scripture is on the family as God's core resource for relationship building and for meeting needs.

The early church had a large percentage of unmarried women in their midst. Caring for them became a problem, and so Paul gave to Timothy some specific instructions for meeting their needs. Each unmarried woman was to be cared for by her family and encouraged to remarry. Failure for a family to care for its own was judged as worse than being unbelievers.

The corporate church limited itself to only caring for those unmarried women who met the following qualifications from 1 Timothy 5:3-14: They had to be widowed, they had to really be in need, and the widow had to be a woman of prayer. They also had no family to care for them—meaning grown children or grandchildren. Plus, the widow had to be over sixty years of age. A widow had to have been faithful to her husband, and the widow had to have a reputation for good deeds—being a godly mother, showing hospitality, serving other believers, and helping those in trouble.

Women who did not meet the above qualifications were encouraged to marry. The admonishment to remarry is not often popular in a culture where Hollywood has dictated romantic love as the prerequisite for marriage. However, Scripture places the prerequisite of marriage as seeking a godly spouse, assuming that real love grows out of the actions of a commitment to God and family.

Many cultures today still arrange marriages and find that love grows out of such a committed relationship. Cultures that have promoted romantic love as a prerequisite for marriage have found that marriage is no longer greatly respected, as divorce rates have gone up and more couples choose to just live together, rather than enter a marriage covenant.

Please note: This is not a teaching on arranged marriages! It is also not an admonition for women to remain at home. Many single and married women today seek fruitful careers and are blessed by God in their endeavors. The point is simply that our priorities are often out of step with God's. His priority is always family and the generations.

Up until one hundred years ago, family and remarriage were the only avenues of help for someone in need. Folks didn't think it odd to remarry for material and family security. Death in childbirth was common and many men had several wives over a lifetime. Men and women who didn't marry lived their whole lives with other family members. Many generations often lived together under one roof, and old folks died in their family home surrounded by relatives, rather than in a nursing home. Talk about working out relationship problems! Believers had no choice but to learn to work on their issues!

It is within a family that the love of God is shown to people in need. Many churches host small groups that meet in homes. These groups often become the extended family to those who have no family of origin to help them. Only after all these family resources have been exhausted does the corporate church step in to help an individual. At that point, the corporate church must make the distinction between the poor and the lazy, because we are commanded to help the poor, but not to help the lazy.

All this is stated to stress the importance of family as God's avenue for meeting needs. This must be re-emphasized in a society where a state welfare system has replaced this family principle, and the corporate church is often viewed as a spiritual welfare system. State welfare systems should be used when needed! The corporate church should help to look after people in need because Jesus commanded us to help the poor. However, His first recourse in meeting needs is within the family and through individuals, rather than the corporate church. If we neglect this principle, then we run the risk of His church becoming a corporation and an institution rather than the family of God.

Helping someone through the grieving process

A friend of ours in another community experienced the sudden death of her young husband. As could be expected, she and the children were devastated. Her friends at church did not know how to respond to the horror of the death. They showed up at the funeral, but otherwise remained at a distance. The people who helped her family through this difficult time were her mother and a Mormon neighbor. Sadly, her church leadership had not prepared its people to care for those in grief.

Grief is natural, although it is never fun. It signals the loss of something that will probably never be recovered. Any kind of loss will invoke grief, such as the death of a loved one, the loss of a job, a move to a new community, or even the end of a ministry. However, it is usually within the context of death that we most expect to encounter grief.

Unfortunately, many of us have never had to face death as our forefathers did. One hundred years ago, death was a part of daily life. When a family member died, they were *laid out* in the parlor for *viewing* by family and friends. It was these family and friends who helped the mortician clean and dress the body. People knew what death looked liked and how to process it. Today, the dead are removed at once to the mortuary where all the preparations are done for the family. The viewing is often formal as family and friends meet in a strange place to look at someone who, in death, appears unlike the loved one.

As a result, many Christians do not know how to process death or walk with someone through the process of grieving. Yet, this is one of our highest callings—to weep with those who weep. The following are guidelines for helping someone deal with bereavement:

> ➤ Allow the person to express their emotions. Do not pressure them to express their feelings if they are not comfortable with doing so. Expect intermittent outpouring of crying, anger, or withdrawal.

➤ Come out of your own personal comfort zone and be available to listen, talk, baby-sit, or send meals and cards on a regular basis throughout the first year of grieving. Be sensitive to their need to be touched or hugged.

➤ Be a ready listener both for adults and children. People need to talk about their feelings, the details of the death and funeral, memories of the deceased, and the reasons for dying. Gently challenge irrational conclusions. Avoid preaching or using clichés.

➤ Pray for and with the bereaved, and comfort them with the promises of Scripture or words of a song or poem. The promises of God are what often sustain us, and others, through the hard times. Hebrews 6:17-20 tells us that they are the anchor of hope that holds our ship stable through the storms of life. You will find it helpful to memorize the following verses so that they are ready to come out of your spirit when you need them to minister to others through a word or card: Isaiah 43:1-2; 49:14-16; Psalm 32:8; 145:14; and Philippians 4:6-7.

➤ Do not say things like, "Well, he led a full life. It's not as though he were dying young," or, "I know just how you feel," or "Time will heal." Remember, every grief is a very personal agony. Refrain from such comments as, "She died because she was in rebellion toward God," or "It was God's will." We heard of one man who had guilt added to grief when someone from his church expressed their belief that his wife would have been raised from the dead if he had gone to the mortuary and prayed for her.

➤ Keep in mind the stages of the grieving process to aid in your understanding of what a person might be going through: (1) shock over the death, (2) denial of the death, (3) anger at God, the deceased, others, and self, (4) guilt, (5) bargaining with God, (6) withdrawal, (7) searching, and (8) acceptance of the death.

We live in perilous times. Nothing in our future is certain, except Heaven. The world we were born into is not the same world we live in today. Violence is increasing as September 11,

2001, forever changed the way we face the future. Still, men have endured much over the centuries and will endure more before the end comes. Jeremiah addressed his nation concerning their lack of endurance and steadfastness many years ago. His words still ring true today: "If you have raced with men on foot and they have worn you out, how can you compete with horses? If you stumble in safe country, how will you manage in the thickets by the Jordan?" (Jeremiah 12:5 NIV).

Chapter application

1. Describe a time in your life when you have had a challenging relationship that needed patience. Which of the instructions discussed in the section, *How to relate to challenging people*, would have been appropriate in your situation?

2. In what ways has your family of origin and/or your in-laws been a help to you during times of struggle?

3. In what ways has God used your family to help another individual or family?

4. What are your experiences with the grieving process?

Chapter 14

Making Church a Safe Place

"You're doing it again," Patty said, as she pulled me out of the church kitchen. That was the agreed upon signal that I had asked for when she spotted me in my administrative mode—bossing people around and otherwise ignoring them in order to have the church potluck set up to my preferences. She knew I had the tendency to be extremely project-oriented and often neglected the people involved in my projects.

This incident happened many years ago and I have improved greatly in this area, but my friends still hold me accountable for this weak spot in my character. Identifying my danger areas, and having others hold me accountable to address them, has helped to make the church we pastor a safe place for those who choose to fellowship here.

I've also learned to express appreciation in creative ways to those who serve with us. My husband likes to publicly validate the ministry of helps as a spiritual gift with the same importance as the more noticeable spiritual gifts of prophecy or word of knowledge. These are some of the things we do to help provide an atmosphere of security to those who call Father's House their home.

Four vital signs of a healthy church

Spiritual leadership is to care for people in such a way that the people grow up and mature. This means that a church should always feel safe to those who attend. The following are four vital signs of a healthy family or church led by healthy leaders. Curiously enough, these same signs are the essentials for caring for a newborn infant. If the newborn is to develop into a strong healthy child, then the care as prescribed here must be provided. And ditto for the care for God's people.

Feeding: It is constantly the task of godly leadership to feed those under their care with the Word of God. This causes the young believer to grow up into a man or woman of God and become a lethal weapon against darkness.

Protecting: It is the task of spiritual leadership to make church a safe place. This means safety from the assaults of seducing spirits from without, and safety from the attacks by misguided and fleshly people within. Church is also to be a place that provides the protection of being accountable to others for the walking out of the Christian life in a manner that brings honor to God.

Exercising: It is the purpose of every church leadership team to equip and train those under their care to do the work of ministry. The leadership is in place to support people in their particular ministries. Church is a place where each person discovers his gifts and callings. The church leadership is then to help equip and launch people into what Jesus is calling them to do.

Resting: A safe church is a place of rest. Many come into the fellowship broken in spirit, soul, and body because of the intense warfare of these days or because of freshly coming out of darkness. At this point, people don't need to be put to work in the church program. What they do need is a lot of love, counseling, and healing. When the church does this, it becomes a true shelter of rest for the weary—a place where people are built up and encouraged by prayer, a hug, or a word of counsel.

Family dynamics

A church is simply a smaller unit of the Family of God. It is made up of people in various stages of maturity. Each has his expectations of what church is to be like, usually projecting his past experience of church or family onto the current fellowship experience. These viewpoints can be hazardous if the individual had a negative childhood. Some might even view the church as a corporation or institution. The concept of a healthy family atmosphere has to be continually taught to a community of believers for the church to be a safe place for all.

In our fellowship, we encourage all members and require all leadership to take a course that teaches the principles in this book. Throughout the year, these principles are referred to in various ways in sermons and other teachings. Accountability is ongoing as folks are encouraged to help one another grow in these values. Parents teach them to their children; couples practice them in their marriages.

As mentioned earlier, our various ministry teams operate with these teachings as foundational beliefs. In fact, each ministry team leader conducts a heart check with the whole team before entering into any kind of ministry. It is viewed as a time of accountability. Anyone with offense problems, unresolved issues with another, or attitude problems, steps off the team for that time of ministry until he has processed his stuff according to scriptural instructions.

Following is a checklist that helps us gauge the ongoing safety of the church we pastor. We encourage anyone who has finished the course on relationships to use this checklist for a periodic check-up concerning their own relational health and that of the fellowship.

✓ I realize that what each contributes to the church family must be sourced from what is flowing out of their personal experience with the Lord. Therefore, I will nurture that relationship as the most important thing in my life.

✓ I refuse to be dysfunctional—I will communicate! I know I am stuck with these people for the rest of eternity, so I'd rather deal with conflict now than have to face Jesus with it someday.

✓ I will not presume that communication has happened just because there has been a discussion.

✓ I will not jump to conclusions or assume anything. I will graciously ask questions and seek to get to the bottom of an issue about which I am concerned.

✓ I will practice reconciliation principles and the instructions on remaining free of offense.

✓ I will make myself available to answer questions and process stuff for which others are concerned.

✓ I will seek to know people's giftings, passion, and skill levels, and accommodate myself accordingly when working with them.

✓ I will encourage genuine relationships that glue people together. When involved in ministry, I will focus on the importance of right relationships during ministry as well as on the activity itself.

✓ I understand that whatever ministry I am involved in is simply a smaller unit of the church, which is not an institution but a living organism. Therefore, I refuse to regard any ministry team as a club or a program, but as a group of people who are each in a constant process of change and growth.

✓ I will not be afraid to say, "Oops, I missed it!" I know that my acceptance and value is not based on my performance or giftings, but on my worth as a member of the Family of God. Therefore, I will encourage input and correction so that I might better my skills and character.

✓ I know that the leadership of the church is based on maturity and godly character, not on the degree of giftedness or skills.

✓ I will not get hung up on ministry titles. I will remember that Jesus was the only one with a title on His team and it was Teacher.

✓ I will look for evidences of God's presence in my church, not evidences of His absence.

Leadership dynamics

In addition, we also provide a checklist for various leaders in our fellowship. This list is a helpful reference tool to use in evaluating a leader if you are considering becoming part of a church or ministry team. Remember, though, that leaders are in a process of development and will still be learning to incorporate the following principles into their leadership role. Ministry leaders and team members can discuss this list together periodically to see if each leader is progressing in his leadership skills. This kind of evaluation is a form of accountability by a leader to his followers and is part of the principle of mutual submission.

✓ As a leader, I will communicate all of the above family dynamics to my followers and model them. I will continue to communicate them in some fashion on a regular basis.

✓ As a leader, I will strive to model Jesus to my followers in everything I do. I will remember that I am always a servant, no matter what my title.

✓ When appropriate, I will use job descriptions to help clarify boundary lines and expectations of various responsibilities of those under my authority.

✓ As a leader, I will communicate to my team what the purpose and goals of the ministry are, such as in a mission statement. This will help to keep the ministry headed in the right direction.

✓ As a leader, I will openly practice all the principles of reconciliation and restoration.

✓ As a leader, I will openly practice and model all the principles of keeping free of offense.

✓ As a leader, I will seek to earn the spiritual authority needed to go with my title of authority through building relationships and trust with those under my care. I will shun demand authority.

✓ As a leader, I will seek to incorporate a plurality of leadership in my ministry.

✓ As a leader, I will practice mutual submission with the people involved in my ministry and actively seek ways to submit to them and their suggestions.

✓ As a leader, I will seek constructive analysis from my team without moving into a self-defense mode or criticizing and excusing their comments.

✓ As a leader, I will constantly seek ways to make this ministry "family."

✓ I will seek creative ways to express appreciation to my ministry team.

Dynamics of church government

Most people become a part of a church fellowship without thinking much about how it is governed. It is only later, when they encounter frustration with leadership, that they begin to investigate the type of government by which the church operates. One of the ways to make church a safe place is to clearly communicate the style of administration that the fellowship embraces. Folks can then adapt themselves accordingly.

Jesus never left His disciples with a *Policy and Procedure Manual* for church government. He expected them to abide by the instructions He had given them for relationships and ministry. Man has incorporated different types of church government to help manage a group of people referred to as the church. For our purposes, we will look at church government as various types of teams, for teams are referred to throughout Scripture.

King David had a team of men around him who helped him make military and spiritual decisions. The apostles functioned as a team in the early church and a missionary team can be seen in Paul, Barnabas, and John Mark. Jesus sent His disciples out two-by-two. When Paul writes to the Philippians, he addresses his letter to the deacons and elders, which were a leadership team. In Acts 6, we see a team of deacons serving the Greek widows.

In Acts 15, we see the church of Jerusalem made up of apostles and elders. The discussion of Gentile circumcision was held within that group and that team reached a corporate decision. It can be noted that within that group was also a team of people consisting of a pastor (James), an apostle (Paul), an evangelist (Peter), and a prophet (John), with all four functioning as teachers. This is a good example of a five-fold ministry team spoken of in Ephesians 4:11-12.

Other examples of various leadership teams and ministry teams are: eldership, home or cell groups, prayer teams, counseling teams, healing ministry teams, worship teams, youth teams, and mission teams. The scriptural concept of leadership rests not on one person, but on a plurality of leadership. It is a shared leadership. This is why the principle of mutual submission is so important in Scripture.

Every group will have a "head leader" because leadership is a spiritual principle. Leadership brings order. Within the Trinity, the Father is the recognized leader. In a marriage, the husband is called the head of the union. In a church, a pastor and elders are leaders. Parents are the leaders of their children. A boss is in leadership over his employee. A worship team needs a leader to bring harmonization of the various members of the worship team, both musically and relationally! A home group will have a leader, even if his role is limited to such as offering his home, setting times to meet, and coordinating the activities of the home group.

When people lack a head leader, confusion results. So, where there is no leader in a group, one will arise. This is true even in small groups of two or three prayer partners. Someone will always take the lead and either make decisions or encourage the group to make decisions, such as where to meet and what the consensus is on what God is speaking to the group. Such leadership should be shared, but at any given point in time someone will be in head leadership. Christian marriage is a good example of where the husband is to be the head, but a plurality of leadership between the husband and wife is expected.

In college, I belonged to a Bible study and prayer group that prided itself in having no leader. We believed it was godly to just let the Holy Spirit be the leader. It never occurred to us that it was a scriptural principle for the Holy Spirit to work through leadership and through those under such leadership! We were oblivious to the fact that it was the Holy Spirit who had authored leadership and inspired the instructions in Scripture concerning leadership. Actually, what we should have been seeking was a plurality of leadership with one person taking responsibility as the head leader, even if all he did was to help bring order to our confusion.

Everyone came to our group gatherings with something to share that the Holy Spirit had given him or her. It could be a song, a Scripture, a teaching, or a prophecy. This was a scriptural practice. However, the group dissolved after a few months, out of frustration. We had an agreement that the evening would conclude with prayer. The prayer time would be ended when we felt it was time to sing *Amazing Grace*, and anyone could take the lead as they felt led.

Unfortunately, one young lady always felt led to start singing *Amazing Grace* just as our prayers began to really break through. There was no one with authority to give correction because to do so would have been to challenge what the Holy Spirit was leading her to do. We also found that prophecies were not judged, as they should be, because different people felt differently about what was being spoken in prophecy. No one had the authority to bring final correction and clarity without someone getting offended. This led to confusion and frustration—fast!

I learned the hard way that God moves within structure. Throughout the Bible, we see God setting up principles of structure that provide order and freedom for His people. It is within order and structure that true freedom can be experienced, because boundaries are clearly defined and they provide a sense of security to those within the boundaries.

146

Nonetheless, people come onto a ministry team with different understandings of what "team" means. A ministry team can mean various things depending on a person's past experience with teams. Combining several people with diverse definitions of what spiritual government is supposed to be is an open door for offense. Confusion often results, with frustration following close behind. Therefore, it is important to understand the structure of a team, what the various roles are of each team member, the purpose of the ministry team, and what healthy team dynamics look like. All that we have studied thus far in this book can be applied to team ministry, for ministry involves people and carries eternal implications.

The following examples of team structures are scriptural and can be found within the pages of your Bible. However, some work better in different situations, denominations, or ministry organizations than others. Learn to know which type of government structure your church or organization operates with and you will find yourself released into greater ministry and less frustration. This is especially true if you are a ministry team leader!

No designated leader: This type of team structure is often seen in a prayer team, but it is not realistic for a group of more than two or three people. One of Murphy's Laws should state, "Where no leader is designated, one will arise." When a leader does arise, the other members of the team may resent his authority. Gear shifting among the members can also be a hindrance because of undefined roles. A plurality of leadership is sometimes hard to maintain within this style of government because boundaries are not clearly defined, which results in little progress toward team goals. An example of this is the earlier story of my experience with a college prayer group.

A designated leader is *over* the team: In this style of government, a designated leader makes all the decisions. The team is more of a support group that carries out the decisions of the leader. Mutual submission and plurality of leadership are present, but not a priority. Boundaries are stringently defined and maintained. The danger of this type of structure is that the leader can appear to be controlling and the followers can be abused. The advantage of this arrangement is that things usually get done quickly and orderly. Examples of this style of government would be military units, the Catholic Church, and religious cults.

A designated leader is *within* the team: This leader acts as a team coordinator who conducts meetings, often using Robert's Rules of Order. Final decisions rest with the team, usually by a vote. The leader has no more authority than the rest of the group, sometimes less. Mutual submission and a plurality of leadership are practiced to some degree, and boundaries are clearly defined and maintained. The leader is authorized to see that the decisions of the team are carried out. The danger of this type of structure is that the team can appear controlling and the leader can be abused. Examples of this type of government would be your local PTA, a Jewish synagogue, and some Protestant churches.

A designated leader is *among* the team: The leader of this team acts as a visionary, guide, and coordinator who processes decisions with the team. Final decisions rest with the leader, although he or she usually goes with the team suggestions. Mutual submission and a plurality of leadership are practiced. The designated leader often delegates his own authority to others more qualified than himself and defers to their decisions. Boundaries are defined but are often loose, as in a family. The team and its leader act together to carry out decisions. The danger present in this style of government is the discomfort of gear shifting for the leader and team as the plurality of leadership develops and grows. Examples of this structure are some Protestant churches, Christian marriage, and many ministry teams.

Whatever style of government a church offers, we need to seek to honor the One who will forever govern us. Only then will our sheep shed be a safe place for His sheep. "For to us a child is born, to us a son is given, and the government will be on his shoulders. And he will be called Wonderful Counselor, Mighty God, Everlasting Father, Prince of Peace. Of the increase of his government and peace there will be no end. He will reign on David's throne and over his kingdom, establishing and upholding it with justice and righteousness from that time on and forever. The zeal of the LORD Almighty will accomplish this" (Isaiah 9:6-7 NIV).

Chapter application

1. Can you identify with church being a place of feeding, safety, resting, and exercise? How?

2. Read over the checklist for "family dynamics" to see how healthy you are in your church relationships.

3. Read over the checklist for "leadership dynamics" to see how healthy you are as a leader and to gauge the health of your church leadership.

4. What is the style of government by which your church operates? What style are you most comfortable with on a church ministry team?

About the Author

When asked what she does, Susan Gaddis replies, "I help people build their spiritual legacies. I mentor them in life skills that translate into an intentional walk of faith, which will pass on, like a baton, to family, friends, and co-workers. Those individuals can grab hold and run with this legacy now and long after the believer's portion of the race is finished. A spiritual legacy should be a clear record of a person's walk of faith, communicating that living for Jesus and being empowered by His grace is more than enough." All of Susan's books, courses, and blog posts relate to building a positive, powerful, spiritual legacy.

Susan Gaddis grew up on a California ranch as the oldest of four children, which taught her the importance of family, fun, and responsibility. Her memories include egg fights in the barn, swimming in cow troughs, lots of hard work, and building tree forts. High School was a mixture of band practice and football games. Susan met her future husband, Tom, in drama class; she believes some academics were thrown in somewhere. She devoured library books and still considers reading her favorite recreational activity.

After finishing L.I.F.E. Bible College, Tom and Susan returned to the Central Coast and have pastored Father's House, a Foursquare Church in Atascadero, CA, ever since. Six children and a number of grandchildren later, they are still learning what it means to be spiritual people. It is Susan's firm belief that, "God gives us a family so our dysfunctional attitudes will rise to the surface where he can address them. Then he blesses us with grandchildren as a way of sweetening the process."

As one of the staff pastors at Father's House, Susan directs the Ministry Training Center and the Counseling Team as well as guides the women's ministry, Forever Girlfriends.

Susan is the author of several books including the *Eternal Foundations for a New Generation* series and *Intercessors, God's End-time Vanguard; How to Pray Effectively for the Things That Matter Most*. During her years in ministry, Susan's articles have been published in *Ministry Today, Advance Magazine, The Teaching Home,* and for Foursquare Women International. She is the past editor of the newsletter Tender Touch, published for pastors' wives on the Western District of Foursquare Churches.

As a conference and retreat speaker, Susan teaches on a variety of subjects including relationships, spiritual disciplines, intercession, contemplative prayer, leadership, and parenting.

When not writing or busy with church responsibilities, Susan enjoys her grandchildren, scrapbooking, gardening, and a cafe' mocha from the Starbucks down the road.

Discover other titles by Susan Gaddis at:

http://www.eternalfoundations.com

Amazon.com

Connect with Susan Online:

Susan's author website: www.susangaddis.net

Holy in the Daily blog: www.susangaddis.net/blog

"Building a Spiritual Legacy" newsletter:

www.cternalfoundations.com/contact

Facebook: http://facebook.com/authorsusangaddis

(Give her Facebook page a "Like" and join the community of people learning how to build a spiritual legacy by encountering the Holy in the daily.)

Twitter: @susangaddis

Linkedin: http://www.linkedin.com/in/susandgaddis

For new releases and resources visit Susan's Eternal
Foundations website at: http://www.eternalfoundations.com

Notes

Chapter 1

[i] Frank B. Minirth, M.D. and Paul D. Meier, M.D., *Happiness is a Choice* (Baker Book House, 1978) 104

Chapter 9

[ii] Jerry Bridges, *The Practice of Godliness* (Navpress, 1983)

[iii] Ibid., 226

Chapter 10

[iv] Clinton, Dr. J. Robert, *The Making of a Leader* (Navpress, 1988) 14